BUSINESS IN CARTOONS

A PRACTICAL GUIDE TO BUSINESS SUCCESS FROM TWO CEOS WHO HAVE SEEN IT ALL

PAUL R. NIVEN AND TOR INGE VASSHUS

ISBN: 978-82-303-4746-1 (Paperback)
ISBN: 978-82-303-4875-8 (Digital)

Editor and Art Director Hana Emma Ramos
Illustrations by Jonathan Brown

Printed by Livonia Print Ltd., in Latvia.

First printing edition 2021.

info@corporater.com

Corporater AS
Hillevågsveien 24
4016 Stavanger
Norway

www.corporater.com

CONTENTS

STRATEGIC PLANNING & EXECUTION

PERFORMANCE & OKR

GOVERNANCE

MANAGING CHANGE

MANAGEMENT & LEADERSHIP

ABOUT THE AUTHORS

DEDICATION

We believe that every person in the world deserves to
be loved and live a happy, healthy life.
We believe that by giving our time, resources and energy we can
bring life where life seems lost, bring light where there is darkness,
and bring increase where things seem to decrease.
We would like to thank and dedicate this book to everyone who actively
strives to create a positive impact on the lives of those in need.

All proceeds from sales of this book will be donated to Seb's Projects India.
For more details and to donate to the cause, please visit www.sebsprojectsindia.org.

INTRODUCTION

Running a successful business takes a lot of work, a lot of skills, and a lot of perseverance. It's like running an endless marathon where the slope, terrain, and weather conditions constantly change. There are sure to be ups and downs, obstacles, and plenty of competitors to be on the lookout for. All we can do to stay in the race is be prepared to the best of our abilities. And that's where knowledge sharing comes into play.

> *Good advice is priceless. Not what you want to hear, but what you need to hear. Not imaginary, but practical. Not based on fear, but on possibility. Not designed to make you feel better, designed to make you better. Seek it out and embrace the true friends that care enough to risk sharing it. I'm not sure what takes more guts — giving it or getting it.* — Seth Godin

We are big fans of receiving the kind of counsel Godin notes, and also sharing our own business advice and expertise with others. We also believe that good points and lessons are often best illustrated through humor. There is a lot that we've learned over the past two decades of consulting with large firms and running our own businesses, and we're excited to share some of our learnings with you in this book. We hope that our stories and tips will come in handy whether you're an experienced business professional or a newbie entrepreneur preparing for your first marathon.

Best,
Paul & Tor Inge

STRATEGIC PLANNING & EXECUTION

WHY YOU NEED A MISSION STATEMENT

"Maybe we shouldn't ask the interns to write our mission statement."

We live in a cultural time that is defined by many things, but unquestionably one of the guiding principles today is the notion that finding your true mission is vital should you hope to lead a happy and productive life. Open any bestselling book, listen to successful people in virtually any field, and their advice will be the same: Find your passion, your mission, and happiness and inner peace will surely follow. An hour before writing this, one of us heard retired female auto racing pioneer Danica Patrick issue this exact counsel. Or was it Richard Branson … or Mark Zuckerberg? You get the picture.

Strangely enough, as accepted as finding your mission is in our personal lives, it is universally derided in the organizational world. Bring up the topic of mission in the halls of your company and you're as likely to be greeted by eye rolls and mentions of a Dilbert cartoon as you are with sincere interest and enthusiasm. But why is this the case? While many concepts we pursue in our personal lives would not translate in the organizational realm, mission does. It is every bit as important for companies as it is for individuals. David Packard, one of the co-founders of Hewlett-Packard, recognized that truth when he delivered this message to employees way back in 1960: "A group of people get together and exist as an institution that we call a company so they are able to accomplish something collectively that they could not accomplish separately — they make a contribution to society … do something which is of value."[i] Inspirational stuff!

Ready to rethink the idea of mission? Great, let's define the term. A mission statement describes the core purpose of the organization — why it exists. The mission examines the *raison d'etre* for the organization beyond simply increasing shareholder wealth, and reflects employees' motivations for engaging in the company's work. The mission attempts to capture the contribution and value that Mr. Packard so eloquently describes, illuminating the core purpose that draws us to our work and inspires our very best.

If you don't have a mission statement, or you require a liberal dose of lemon Pledge to get the dust off your current mission, here are some tips to get you started on outlining yours.

1. *Ask "why" you exist*

   And not just once. Maybe three, four, or even five times, until you unearth why it is you exist. Your first round might yield responses such as, "To provide shareholders with a fair return on their investment," or "To provide (insert product or service here) to our customers." Yawn. Will those stale bromides get people bouncing out of bed in the morning? Not likely. Keep asking why until you discover what it is that really gets your juices flowing.

2. *Write it for the long term*

   Strategies may change over time. In fact, they should evolve as circumstances in your operating environment dictate. The mission, however, should be written to stand the test of time. It should remain the bedrock of the organization, serving as the stake in the ground for all future decisions.

3. *Make it easily understood and communicated*

   Simplicity reigns when it comes to mission statements. A compelling and memorable mission is one that reaches people on a visceral level, speaks to them and motivates them to serve the organization's purpose. Forget the buzzwords, and put away the thesaurus for this exercise. Focus on honesty and authenticity.

Call us idealistic, but we believe David Packard's words are true; people do want to make a difference. However, the global statistics on employee engagement are currently dismal to say the least. Our contention is that engagement is suffering not because people don't like what they're doing, but because they've lost sight of (or were never introduced in the first place) to why they're doing it. A mission statement holds the promise of creating that line of sight and is a vital first step in ensuring all members of your team are actually rowing in the same direction.

Source:

[i] James C. Collins and Jerry I. Porras, "Building Your Company's Vision," *Harvard Business Review*, September–October, 1996.

PUTTING CLARITY INTO YOUR VISION STATEMENT

"That's our vision statement. Our management likes to keep it real."

At some point in our careers, we've all seen vision statements that attempt to fire up employees with inspiring words like "best," "greatest," or "biggest." The problem is that without context, those words are flat, empty, and open to endless interpretation. How do we know when we're the best, greatest, or biggest? To really ignite employees' imagination and innovation, a vision must go beyond superlative adjectives and provide a true destination that people can see and work toward.

An authentic vision statement provides a word picture of what the organization intends ultimately to become — which may be five, ten, or fifteen years in the future. The statement should not be abstract — it should contain as concrete a picture of the desired state as possible, including a quantitative destination. When Muhtar Kent assumed the CEO position at Coca-Cola, he was asked about his top priority moving forward. Without hesitation he replied, "Establishing a vision … a shared picture of success. We call it 2020 vision and it calls for us to double the business in ten years. It's not for the fainthearted but it's clearly doable." That is a vision! Clear, compelling, time-bound, and quantitative. Improve your vision statement with these tips.

1. *Keep it short*

   The best vision statements grab our attention and stay with us because they communicate volumes in just a few words. Look again at Coca-Cola's 2020 vision — double the business in ten years. Anyone can grasp and easily recall that statement. There is a direct correlation between the number of words in a vision statement and how well it is understood and acted on. More words, more confusion.

2. *Ensure it's feasible*

   The goal in crafting a vision statement is to inspire employees to hitherto unimaginable levels of performance. However, there is a point at which the arc of inspiration bends toward the absurd and impossible. If you publish a vision with numbers that are clearly unachievable given your current prospects, it will lead to skepticism and disdain. Rigorous analysis of your situation should lead to the creation of a vision that balances breakthrough performance with unvarnished reality.

3. *Make sure it's quantitative*

   One more time, the purpose of the vision is to create a word picture of your desired future. A growth target, a certain number of customers, entry into new markets, or any other myriad possibilities may encapsulate your desired future. Without a quantitative destination, employees are left groping in virtual darkness, uncertain of which direction to head in when apparently any will suffice.

In *Undaunted Courage*, his outstanding chronicle of the Lewis and Clark expedition of 1803, author Stephen Ambrose notes the great lengths taken by the two leaders to inspire their corps of discovery. And it worked. As Ambrose notes:

> *The men of the expedition were linked together by uncommon experiences and by the certain knowledge that they were making history, the realization that they were in the middle of what would without question be the most exciting and important time of their lives, and the obvious fact that they were in all this together, that every man was dependent on all the others, and they on him.*

Imagine being able to harness the creative and intellectual power of your teams — the unprecedented heights you could reach. It's there for the taking, and starts with the creation of a crystallizing vision.

CREATING CLARITY WITH A STRATEGIC DESTINATION STATEMENT

"We picked Hawaii as our strategic destination."

Have you ever heard about a strategic destination statement? Not many people have, and not many organizations have one. Perhaps it's because mission and vision statements are already two too many to remember. Strategic destination statement can, however, be quite useful. Allow us to elaborate.

A strategic destination statement is like a vision statement with a clearly articulated long-term description of the desired state of an organization at a particular future point in time. For instance, in 3-5 years. It typically includes positional descriptive sentences about the areas and aspects of your business that you can control, such as sales, markets, finances, profit, products, processes, people, competence, and systems. The statement is quantifiable and tells *what* the future success looks like. At its core, it doesn't focus so much on *how* the business will get to the future state, but rather on the destination itself.

Crafting a strategic destination statement is a good exercise for any company. Simply ask your team: "What does success look like for ABC group in 3-5 years' time? Please articulate it. Don't worry about the *how* we'll get there. Just describe *what* it looks like."

You may receive answers such as:

- ABC group should have an annual ARR turnover of 500 M NOK by 2025
- Income from M&A should not account for more than 50% of our growth
- Sales from partners should be 80% of our annual turnover by 2025
- Revenue should come mostly from our new GRC offering
- We will raise 800 M NOK over the next 4 years to do strategic M&A
- ABC is owned by employees (60%), 30% external, 10% VC by 2025
- ABC group will create a marketplace for 3rd party vendors to sell their services by 2024

- ABC group will be able to re-package the software platform to our partner's brand by 2023

Once your team aligns on the *what*, they may start brainstorming on the *how* and other details to arrive at a complete version of your strategic destination statement. A complete strategic destination statement includes details related to what will be achieved, why, when, how, for who, and through what means.

Here is an example:

> *Eager Beaver & Son, Inc. will increase its beaver dam footprint in Norway by 2 percent to keep beaver communities safe from predators. By 2022 it will develop a program for ongoing education of fellow eager beavers, who want to improve their beaver dam-building skills and play an active role in their beaver community. Eager Beaver & Son, Inc. will differentiate its education program by offering expertise on innovative construction engineering techniques and modern architectural designs.*

Now let's break it down:

Eager Beaver & Son, Inc. Strategic Destination Statement

Who (organization)	Eager Beaver & Son, Inc.
Will do what (action)	will increase its beaver dam footprint in Norway by 2%
Why (reason)	to keep beaver communities safe from predators
By when (timeframe)	By 2022
How (method)	it will develop a program for ongoing education
For who (target market)	fellow eager beavers, who want to improve their beaver dam-building skills and play an active role in their beaver community
Through what (means)	offering expertise on innovative construction engineering techniques and modern architectural designs

Different versions of this breakdown chart exist, but you get the idea. While such a statement might be too long to remember, going through the exercise of developing a strategic destination statement might serve as an eye-opener about your organization's strategic alignment.

In one of his books about Balanced Scorecards and operational dashboards, the author Ron Person shares a story in which chief executive officers tasked their executive teams to fill out a destination statement using a blank chart like the one you see above. The filled-out sheets were then returned to the CEOs. What the CEOs learned is that each executive had a completely different perception about where the organization was heading. There was a notable lack of clarity on the part of the executive teams, and the CEOs had a lot of communicating to do to get everyone on the same page.

We encourage you to try this exercise at your organization. You may discover a lot of surprises.

IS YOUR PRODUCT OR SERVICE REALLY DIFFERENTIATED?

One of the most eye-opening findings we've ever come across in scanning business literature is this one, which identifies the often titanic-sized gap between perception and reality when it comes to what customers really think about a company's products. Researchers surveyed executives across a range of industries and asked if they felt their product or service was differentiated from their competitors. Eighty percent replied in the affirmative, that yes indeed they did supply something different to the market. When the question was put to customers of those same products and services, however, a very different picture emerged. Just 8 percent of customers felt the offering was differentiated. Can you hear it? The sound of senior executives' jaws dropping as the realization of just what a black hole they're operating in finally hits them.

Differentiation is the original and ongoing battleground of competition in any industry. If your product or service is not distinct in some discernible way — either offering different attributes or providing the same attributes in a meaningfully superior way — there is little chance of separating yourself from the competitive herd. It's like being a cover band in music. You can make a living imitating The Rolling Stones, but you'll never top the charts. Here are a few things to consider when determining whether or not your product or service is truly differentiated.

1. *Ask your customers*

    In the spirit of the statistic shared above, the first thing you need to do is get the facts. Survey a subset of customers to determine whether they, the ones who actually give you money, feel your wares stand out from the crowd. What you find may surprise and shock you into action.

2. *Map your value chain*

   This advice is straight from Harvard strategy guru Michael Porter, and you don't need to read one of his lengthy tomes to take advantage of it. Simply examine the processes you employ for critical activities, including product or service design, production, sales, and support. Do they differentiate from your competitors in any kind of significant way? If not, it's time to hit the whiteboard with ideas.

3. *Look at the numbers*

   Hopefully, you're tracking a balanced set of metrics across your organization that includes customer yardsticks. If so, examine the trends carefully. Market share, customer retention, customer satisfaction, net promoter score, and so on. If you're seeing the needle move in the wrong direction on these and other indicators, chances are your products are no longer seen as differentiated in the eyes of customers.

To keep your customers from beating a path to your competitors, cast a critical eye on whether you really are differentiating in a consequential way. And to give the exercise the gravitas it deserves, keep in mind the words of Walmart founder, Sam Walton: "There is only one boss — the customer. And he can fire everybody in the company from the chairman on down simply by spending his money somewhere else."

Sources:

The statistic on executive and customer perceptions of differentiation is from Chris Zook and James Allen, *Repeatability: Building Enduring Businesses for a World of Constant Change*. Boston, MA., Harvard Business School Press, 2012.

The value chain concept has been examined in many sources. We drew from Joan Magretta, *Understanding Michael Porter: The Essential Guide to Competition and Strategy*. Boston, MA., Harvard Business School Press, 2012.

THE IMPORTANCE OF STRATEGIC AGILITY

"We have a strategy, so what's the problem?"

Corporate lifespans are shrinking dramatically. Back in 1958 the average tenure of a company on the S&P 500 was sixty-one years. It dropped to twenty-five years by 1980. Today it's down to just eighteen. Those numbers demonstrate that growth and sustainability are not guaranteed in today's warp speed, hyper-competitive global economy. Back in the relatively stable 1950s, organizations could perhaps afford to create a "set it and forget it" strategy that would pay dividends over years, if not decades. Not so today.

The modern enterprise, locked in a constant battle for competitive advantage, must embrace the concept of strategic agility. This entails contemplating and revising its strategy frequently, based on constant sensing and rapid adaptation to stimuli in its competitive orbit. Try these tips to improve your strategic agility.

1. *Use the wisdom of the crowd*

   At the end of the day, your senior leadership must assume the responsibility for crafting the organization's strategy. However, this responsibility doesn't mean they are omniscient beings blessed with a crystal ball showing the future in perfect detail. Given the tools available to even small organizations today, you should tap the wisdom of all employees — especially those close to customers — to glean their insights as to the best strategic directions to follow. One simple tool to employ is a "strategy jam." Create a page on your intranet to collect strategy ideas and invite employees to contribute during a defined period of time — the "jam." Collect the ideas and use them as raw materials when crafting strategy.

2. *Explain the importance of strategy*

   As noted above, in most organizations strategy setting is the exclusive purview of the leadership team. Therefore, many employees will ignore the concept altogether, assuming strategy is something that is created behind closed boardroom doors that will ultimately bear little relevance for their day-to-day actions. In today's world nothing could be further from the truth. Every employee, especially those deemed as "knowledge workers," must understand that they play a key role in gathering strategic information and feeding it up the ladder so that it can be assimilated quickly and translated into action. The old paradigm of holding a town hall meeting to announce your three- or five-year strategy to a less-than-enthusiastic audience of overwhelmed employees is dead. You must communicate both the importance of strategy and your specific priorities constantly to ensure all employees recognize it as a core part of their job.

3. *Embrace the lean revolution*

   The concepts of lean management, exemplified by the Toyota Production System, have gained traction, and demonstrated benefits, in virtually all industries. If your goal is to introduce agility into your strategy process, facilitating possible changes in product and service mix, methods of distribution, and so on, you must ensure all downstream processes in your organization are themselves agile and lean — always adding value for customers while eliminating waste. There are many excellent books, white papers, and conferences celebrating the lean movement, thus a good first step is to simply learn more about the fundamentals of the topic and how it may be applied effectively in your own organization.

How often do you update your strategic plan? Depending on the life cycle of your industry, if it's more than two years, it may be too infrequent. We'll leave you with the guidance of strategy and change guru John Kotter:

> *Companies used to reconsider their strategies only rarely. Today any company that isn't ... constantly adjusting to changing contexts — and then quickly making significant operational changes is putting itself at risk ... Strategy should be viewed as a dynamic force that constantly seeks opportunities.*

Couldn't have said it better ourselves!

Sources:

Corporate life span statistics from Clark Gilvert, Matthew Eyring, and Richard N. Foster, "Two Routes to Resilience," *Harvard Business Review*, December 2012.

Kotter quote: From *Harvard Business Review.*

BEWARE THE "BEST"

Back in the early 1980s, when we were both fresh-faced college students, all the "cool kids" in class were toting copies of *In Search of Excellence,* the Peters and Waterman tome destined to become the first true business blockbuster and a must-have on the credenza of every credible executive. The mere ability to parrot a few choice passages or tell the simplified tale of one of its exemplary companies awarded one with a certain cachet and prestige both in and out of class. Later, when we were in corporate jobs, it was *Built to Last*, then *Reengineering the Corporation*, and later *Good to Great*. There were many others as well.

Reflecting back on all those many pages, what stands out are not only the lessons imparted by the gurus of each successive age, but the repetition in the use of certain companies to "prove" their particular theory of choice. It didn't matter whether it was reengineering, strategy development, lean thinking, or enterprise performance management. Regardless of the principle, the same companies were used again and again. When we were starting out, writers were erecting statues in ink for the likes of Atari and Xerox. Later it was Enron and Dell (and we know what happened to Enron), and now the darlings appear to be (among others) Apple, Google, Amazon, and Facebook.

Amazon, Apple, Google, Facebook and the other stars shining in the business galaxy today are unquestionably successful companies, but it's both dangerous and unfair to emulate them with singular devotion and expect the rewards to suddenly rain down on you. All of these companies perform a specific combination of activities that act together in a synergistic way to drive the execution of their strategies. If we could all copy everything they do, we would, but it's obviously not that simple. Nor should you want to follow blindly what others do.

Here are three healthy ways to keep an eye on other organizations, without blind devotion to them:

1. *Monitor but don't necessarily copy*

   We hear it every day: things are changing more rapidly than ever. Therefore, it's incumbent on every business to keep track of changes in all facets of life: technology, demographics, socio-political, and so on. If you see a company doing cool and innovative things, by all means examine it, but think carefully about your particular situation before adopting their approach.

2. *Determine where you need help*

   Chances are that some areas of your business require more pressing attention than others. If one function in particular is struggling, look to the "stars" of that field and consider adopting any proven best practices. For example, Walmart is a good place to start if you're plagued with supply chain and logistics woes.

3. *Run small experiments*

   Before investing in a full implementation of what seems to be working at another company, try it as a pilot project within your firm. Document the experience and determine whether a wider rollout is merited.

There is an enormous gap between admiring and learning from a company versus trying to copy its success. It's healthy and productive to learn from others, but you still need to apply a liberal dose of homegrown wisdom and know-how forged in the battles that shaped *your* unique culture if you hope to achieve success yourself.

HOW TO KNOW YOU'RE NOT SERIOUS ABOUT STRATEGY EXECUTION

"I'm 100% behind it, but I'm swamped. Who can run with this?"

Every time one of us gets an inquiry from a potential new client, it triggers a little dopamine hit. It's always interesting and exciting to open an email from a prospect: Where are they from? What industry are they in? What prompted them to reach out and learn more about our respective services? But the dopamine rush gets whisked away in an instant when the inquiry reads something like this:

"Hi, I'm Ashley, the CEO's admin assistant. He asked me to reach out to companies like yours because we're interested in learning more. Can you please send me a list of your services and prices?"

We're not taking shots at Ashley here. She (and just as often it's a Jim or Justin FYI) is just doing her job, following up on her boss's wishes. We are, however, suggesting this is a less than ideal way to start a relationship with a potential provider, whether for consulting services or software. It sounds cliché, we know, but every client is different and will require a customized mix of services in order to reach their specific goals. You're not buying a T-shirt online here, folks. When selecting a partner, if your only basis for the choice is a bare menu of prices and services, you're depriving yourself of the value that comes from a true partnership between provider and client. And, frankly, it demonstrates a lack of commitment on the prospect's part if they can't even summon up the interest to hold a conversation with potential providers.

Let's turn this around — here are three things any CEO or leader should do when selecting a potential consulting or software partner:

1. *Conduct research on the topic*

   Know what you're buying! And, backing up from that, an even more basic question to ask is this: Why are you buying? What is the specific business reason you have for reaching out to a consulting or software partner? What is the problem you're trying to solve? Only by answering that question can you make an informed choice based on what the market has to offer.

2. *Go beyond the sticker*

   Don't ever select a partner solely on the lowest price. On the rarest of occasions, you'll get lucky and find a firm whose low prices are not representative of a lack of skill or experience. But for the most part, the old axiom fits: You get what you pay for. Deep subject matter expertise, relevant experience, and cultural fit are the true yardsticks for a healthy relationship between client and provider. Sometimes you'll pay a bit more, but the rewards far outweigh the incremental hit to your P&L.

3. *Don't "outsource" the work*

   This relates to our opening salvo in this chapter — never have an administrative assistant or other person with no decision-making power conduct calls with your potential partner. Chapter one, page one of any book on change management will tell you that senior executive support is the make-or-break ingredient in any initiative. That commitment starts from the day you decide to reach out for some external help. Do it yourself to demonstrate to everyone your personal dedication to selecting the right partner for your specific needs.

We'd love to speak with you if you ever have any need for our services. Just make sure it's you, and not your assistant reaching out.

3 SIGNS YOUR STRATEGY EXECUTION IMPLEMENTATION IS IN TROUBLE BEFORE YOU START

"This is the one!"

Coming together is a beginning. Keeping together is progress. Working together is success.

— Henry Ford

There are potential pitfalls all along the strategy execution path, but some have the potential to derail your efforts before you're even putting marker to flip chart, brainstorming your first objective. Outlined below are three culprits we've seen several times.

1. *"Well, I read the book, and it made sense."*

   "Why are we implementing OKR or Balanced Scorecard, and why now?" is the first question you should ask yourself before embarking on this path. If you answer, "Well, I read (fill in the bestselling book) and it seemed to make sense," then you have a problem. Reading a book and having the message resonate with you is not a valid reason for embarking on any organizational change effort. Your first and greatest obligation when launching a strategy execution program is to share a powerful and meaningful change story to your teams. To do so you must go above and beyond trite, tired, and oft-repeated lines such as "We need to work together more effectively" (everyone knows that already). Instead, weave a broader narrative that outlines how excelling in execution allows you to get closer to customers, offering solutions to their problems, or how strategy execution tools allow everyone the chance to demonstrate their contribution to overall success.

2. *"Over to you, Paul ..." syndrome*

   Our second sign that your implementation is in trouble is less theoretical and more personal for one of us (Paul). "Over to you, Paul" describes a situation that any consultants reading this can surely relate to, and probably dislike as much as I do. Here's the scenario: I'm scheduled to run a training workshop, usually my first interaction with a broader audience at the client's location, at let's say 9:00 a.m. By 9:05 everyone who is going to attend has arrived and, just as I'm expecting the CEO to provide a rousing change story and then introduce me to share the nitty-gritty of how strategy execution can bring that narrative to life, he or she looks at me, and says, "OK." As in "You can start now." No introduction of the concept, why everyone is sacrificing their valuable time, no introduction to this stranger at the front of the room. Nothing. This of course relates to the broader change story theme outlined in our first sign. What kind of a message is this executive sending, when he can't take five minutes to kick off what is supposedly a critical initiative for the organization?

3. *No champion*

   Even if you're fortunate enough to have a CEO willing to take the time and effort to craft a persuasive change story, he or she cannot single-handedly summon the will to make strategy execution a success. Every executive needs a partner; someone who will run the program logistically and philosophically: the in-house subject matter expert. We call this person the "champion" and their role can make or break your implementation. Someone needs to be steering the ship, and that person is the champion. Sure, it will require an investment of that person's time, but if you're not willing to make that investment, you're probably not ready for a successful implementation.

Organizational change and strategy execution are hard enough as it is. The last thing you want to do is handcuff yourself before you even get started.

CONNECT TO STRATEGY

A vision and strategy aren't enough. The long-term key to success is execution. Each day. Every day.
— Richard M. Kovacevich

If you're lucky, you've managed to select some great people as heads of your departments. They're skilled, trustworthy, dependable, loyal, and passionate about their work, and yet you, like many companies out there, might find yourself struggling with strategy execution.

It's not that your team is a bunch of opinionated grumps who can't seem to find common ground. What we often see as a cause of poorly executed company strategy is that department heads get so focused on their department's specific goals that they forget about the big picture.

When we consult with different organizations, we first assess their company goals and objectives, and then we speak with the department heads.

- To the CFO, who is all about numbers, we say: "Budgets and resource allocation are not independent tasks — you need to base your resource allocation on the company's strategic objectives. So, connect with your company's strategy."
- To the quality assurance director, responsible for standards and compliance, we say: "Quality is about doing things right, but what the right things to do are is described in your strategy. So, connect with your company's strategy."
- To the operations/innovation manager, who lives and breathes processes and business process reengineering (BPR), we say: "Process optimization is good, but which processes should you optimize? Connect with your company's strategy."

- When we meet the project manager with a big portfolio of projects to manage, we ask the question: "How do your projects help your company to fulfill its strategy? Have you linked up your portfolio to the company's strategy? If not,— connect with your company's strategy."
- Then we come to the risk manager, who uses risk heat maps as wallpaper, and we ask how they identify risk. "Do you assess only what can go wrong in your surroundings, or do you also consider risks that can prevent the company from fulfilling its goals? You need to connect to strategy when defining risk factors."
- Finally, we come to the HR manager. Their view is that having competent employees is the most important company goal. We tell them that "People and competence is not a goal in itself. It needs to be developed according to what the company is trying to accomplish in its strategy. HR needs to be connected to strategy."

Strategic alignment is the cornerstone of good governance. If your communication skills are on point, it's typically not difficult to get everyone on the same page about what you want to achieve as a company and how you plan to achieve it. The challenge is to get everyone to embrace the strategy and act in accordance with the plan when they go back to their desks. Executing organizational strategy requires time, work, and discipline from everyone (including you!) in your organization. However, it's well worth the effort. Those organizations that are able to successfully connect departmental goals with company strategy will benefit from greater operational efficiency, improved performance, and a greater likelihood of meeting their company goals.

LIVING THE STRATEGY

"Now if you turn to page 136, that's when things really start to get interesting."

Good communication does not mean that you have to speak in perfectly formed sentences and paragraphs. It isn't about slickness. Simple and clear go a long way.

— John Kotter

Are your employees living your company strategy? Do they even know what your company strategy is? If not, you are not alone. What we often hear when speaking with employees from different organizations is that they have zero clue about where their company is heading or what the plan is to get there. It's not that employees don't care. They're simply not kept in the loop.

For employees to live your strategy, you must communicate it. Better yet, if it's feasible, involve your employees in the strategy creation process. Employees will be more likely to carry out your strategy if they help to plan it.

In addition, consider these tips:

1. *Keep it simple.* Articulate your strategy in the simplest way possible, so that employees can immediately understand how it works and what is expected of them.
2. *Visualize it.* Design your strategic plan as an easy-to-follow roadmap that everyone has access to.
3. *Collaborate.* Allow your employees to challenge you with ideas and recognize their input.
4. *Communicate.* Schedule regular strategy review meetings to monitor your progress and keep everyone informed about how your numbers stack up against the plan.

Fostering a workplace environment where employees can partake in the big picture strategy planning is vital for employee buy-in. When employees get to play an active role in the development of a company strategy plan, they're more likely to follow its steps and lead your business to successful outcomes.

WAKE UP TO THE POWER OF CATALYTIC MECHANISMS

"Why does the battery always run out in the middle of the night?!"

Has this ever happened to you? You're lying in bed with your spouse or partner, sleeping peacefully when you're awakened from your slumber by a beeping sound. It probably takes two or three beeps to register, then you're both awake and irritated enough to realize it's repeating in a pattern. Groggy as you are, you soon recognize the culprit: a smoke detector battery that needs — no, it demands — to be changed. Why do these things always decide to go off in the middle of the night?

After the inevitable waiting game, each of you hoping it might miraculously stop or that the other will take care of it, you give in, stumble out of bed, and go in search of the incessant beeping. As annoying as this is, it also provides a great example of a catalytic mechanism. The smoke detector going off forces you into action. There is really no alternative. You have to get out of your cozy bed and change the battery or suffer the severely negative consequences of being robbed of a good night's sleep.

Of course, catalytic mechanisms don't just apply to late-night battery changes. Best-selling business author Jim Collins, who originally wrote about this topic, believes they are crucial for any organization that wants to move beyond bureaucratic exercises in pursuit of their goals. He describes them as the crucial link between objectives and performance. They can take many forms, but the common denominator is a process or procedure that forces people to take direct action in pursuit of an important objective.

Collins cites the case of Granite Rock, a California company that supplies materials and products to the construction industry. When you think of a rock company (and really who isn't constantly doing that) we doubt you conjure up images of world-class customer service. But service at a level exceeding what you might expect at Nordstrom, the American luxury department store chain, was exactly what the leaders of Granite Rock proposed to achieve. To do that they could have written vision statements, created an exciting communication campaign, or devised some complex service initiative, but in the end, they chose one simple process: short pay. At the bottom of every invoice the company issued there appeared a note reading: "If you are not satisfied for any reason, don't pay us for it. Simply scratch out the line item, write a brief note about the problem, and return a copy of this invoice along with your check for the balance." This is a truly catalytic mechanism. Any time a customer chooses not to pay the entire invoice amount it propels Granite Rock into action, digging deep to discover why the customer chose not to fully pay, and doing everything in their power to fix the problem to ensure it doesn't happen again. Employees are provided with a crystal-clear signal that anything less than world-class service won't be tolerated.

We have just one tip/question to offer you when it comes to catalytic mechanisms:

Which of your strategic objectives is so critical to your success that you should attach a catalytic mechanism to it in order to ensure you've fully committed to its achievement? Every objective is important or else it wouldn't be on your radar. However, there is probably one, or maybe two, that rise above the rest, likely representing the clearest indication of your differentiating value proposition. Identify those and create catalytic mechanisms to demonstrate your true commitment. What process could you put in place that would force you to move beyond the corporate rhetoric and turn your dreams into reality?

It takes courage to initiate a catalytic mechanism because a well-constructed version will possess sharp teeth and produce legitimate consequences for the organization should they consistently fall short. The upside, however, is worth the risk. A catalytic mechanism has the power to motivate entire organizations, wow customers, and create sustainable results. What's beeping in your world?

Source:

Notes: http://www.jimcollins.com/article_topics/articles/aligning-action.html

RITUAL RAIN DANCE

"She can't come to the phone for the next six months. She's very busy."

A budget is telling your money where to go instead of wondering where it went.

— John Maxwell

Most large companies start their budgeting process about six months before the start of the financial year. The pre-planning phase typically starts in spring, when the budget's foundations are laid. And the *real* planning then takes place in the fall, when budget decisions are made. During that time period, it's nearly impossible to get people from the finance department to attend seminars, arrange business meetings, or discuss business. They're so busy!

Creating an annual budget is by no means an easy exercise. It can take months to draft and weeks to finalize, especially if your organization still uses manual ways of gathering data. And that's not the only budgeting issue we see in businesses today.

Here are four common budgeting mistakes and how to prevent them:

1. *Carving your budget in stone – "It took us months to create this! Let's not mess with it!"*

   Many organizations today treat budgeting as a *one and done* ordeal. They've gone through the budgeting exercise, everyone is happy with the budget, and no one wants to hear about it again until next year. The reality, however, is that your budget is outdated the moment you write it. There are simply too many unknown internal and external factors that might impact your costs and cash flow throughout the year. Take the 2020 COVID-19 crisis, for instance. Rather than a "let's stick with what we have" attitude, organizations must learn to make continuous budget adjustments to best support their business operations.

2. *Considering your budgets as an "authorization to spend" – "Yes, money! Let's spend it!"*

   Many managers mistakenly consider their budgets as an authorization to spend. They get their budgets approved and off they go — mindlessly spending money left and right as if it was their duty to the company. This can be a value-destroying attitude. If you're granted a budget, make sure to spend it wisely. All your spending decisions should be made with careful consideration. Will your decision lead to more profits? Is it smart? Is it in alignment with the company strategy? Is it necessary?

3. *Missing a good business opportunity because of a lack of budget "We cannot pursue any major growth initiatives. It's not in the budget."*

   Having a lack of budget doesn't translate to "cannot spend." Do not pass on opportunities that are guaranteed to yield profits. If your budget won't quite stretch to the full amount you need, for instance, to develop your department or pursue a large-scale project, share your ideas with the CFO and the rest of the leadership team. If your idea is justified, there might just be some "spare change" in the company's budget bucket. If you don't ask, you will never know.

4. *Using static spreadsheets "But this is how we've always done it."*

   Using static spreadsheets to manage your budget introduces many challenges. Static spreadsheets are often tricky to update — making it difficult for organizations to keep track of their actual spending and revenue. They're also prone to human error and laborious to reconcile when multiple versions exist.

Instead of sticking with the *old way* of doing things, consider investing in a business budgeting software with a real-time visibility and collaboration features. Look for one that links budgets to business objectives, integrates with your existing systems, and allows you to forecast cash flow, track your spending plan, monitor trends, generate reports, respond to market changes, and make strategic spending decisions.

5. *Playing the guessing game "How about if we just guesstimate everything?"*

   Make sure that your company's budgets are based on sound business scenarios and investment decisions. Coming up with budget numbers on a whim will do your business no good. Be diligent, accurate, and realistic when creating budgets, but know that things may change. Throughout the year, if your hypotheses are no longer valid or if your business surroundings are changing,— change the budget.

Having a solid annual budget is often considered as one of an organization's most important financial tools. It provides organizations with the big picture overview of their finances and gives guidance on how to best use their money throughout the year. To stay on top of the budget, it's important for organizations to treat their budget as a *dynamic* plan for the future, embrace the benefits of modern budgeting technology, and approach budgeting as an ongoing, agile activity, not a rain dance ritual that happens once a year.

PERFORMANCE & OKR

Note: In this section we will use the term measure, as you would encounter it in the Balanced Scorecard methodology, interchangeably with the term Key Result, which you would find in the OKR framework.

THE ART OF WRITING AN EFFECTIVE OBJECTIVE

"We're picking our objectives for the year."

A goal properly set is halfway reached.
— Zig Ziglar

Whether you're using the Balanced Scorecard, OKR, or both, your success is highly dependent on the ability of your teams to write technically proficient and effective objectives. Without solid objectives you have about as much chance of seeing the benefits of alignment, transparency, focus, and accountability as you do of winning the lottery without going to the trouble of buying a ticket. It's that important! So, let's break it down.

A well-written objective is comprised of three parts:

1. *A verb.* Objectives are action-oriented, and therefore must start with a verb.
2. *What you're going to do.* This is the aspirational component of the objective.
3. *"In order to" or "so that."* This last piece is critical because it describes the business impact you hope to achieve with the objective.

Here's an example: Reduce mobile app crashes in order to improve the user experience.

Point number three above is really the secret sauce of a great objective. It's relatively easy to open your laptop, start a new document and briskly fill the page with statements starting with a verb and outlining a goal for the future. But the final component, the business impact, is where the true value lies. Your "in order to" or "so that" represents the strategic relevance of your chosen objective, how it will actually propel the organization forward in a desired, and strategic, direction. Articulating your anticipated business impact also paves the way for powerful conversations with your boss. You'll have to cogently defend your choice, and in so doing you'll be sharing your view of the company's strategy. If you've got it right, great! If you don't … that's great too because you can then have a meaningful dialog with your boss on where the company is going, and how you (or your team) fit in.

Beyond sticking to the formula above, effective objectives should be:

- *Meaningful to you.* The more you care about an objective, the more likely you are to achieve it.
- *Aspirational but attainable.* Stretch yourself, but not beyond what's possible.
- *Mostly controllable by the team.* "Mostly," but sometimes you need help with an objective, and that can result in shared objectives, which drive cross-functional collaboration.
- *Doable in the time period.* However, some objectives will roll over to the next period, and that's OK as long as you update your key results.

Take your time, and carefully deliberate when composing objectives. The commitment will pay you back many times over in the form of enhanced execution.

GROW YOUR WAY TO BETTER MEASUREMENT

"The leadership couldn't come up with any real performance measures, so we're being measured by who can tell the best joke."

If you haven't already read the book *You Already Know How to Be Great: A Simple Way to Remove Interference and Unlock Your Greatest Potential* by Alan Fine and Rebecca Merrill, you should do so, immediately. Wait … after you finish this one, of course. Alan has decades of experience coaching world-class athletes, executives, and people from all walks of life looking to elevate their performance to another level. Although there are many terrific tools in the text, the primary mechanism suggested for coaching others is the GROW model, which stands for *goal*, *reality*, *options*, and *way forward*. As the words suggest, we start by outlining the goals, then put them into perspective by recognizing the current reality the person faces. At that point we brainstorm potential options, and finally agree on a preferred way forward.

The model has been used by countless coaches around the world, but in this chapter, we're going to co-opt the phrase for another purpose: Creating better performance measures (or Key Results if using OKRs). Drafting performance measures to gauge success is a task undertaken by virtually every organization on the planet, so you'd think we'd all be pretty good at it by now, but the fact of the matter is we're not. It's not uncommon to struggle with measures that are infrequent, completely irrelevant to the organization's strategy, and ultimately drive the wrong behaviors. Time to GROW up! Let's look at how we can use the acronym to draft better measures.

Goal

The goal is the objective, what we're ultimately striving toward. If you don't have objectives in place (increase customer loyalty, improve manufacturing yield, enhance employee engagement), you're creating measures in a vacuum, and they'll be of little value. So, before you even start thinking about measures, ensure you have an agreed-on set of objectives from which to work. And of course, follow our advice in the previous chapter for creating effective objectives.

Reality

In this step we look at our current reality in the context of the objective. Let's take the example of "Increase customer loyalty to build market share." An obvious measure used to gauge success would be "market share." However, before deciding on that and moving on, you must determine where you currently stand in terms of share. If your customers are defecting in droves, you have no loyalty program or customer relationship management platform, then you've got some issues to figure out. Take some time to document the current situation before advancing to the next step.

Options

Here we examine the objective in light of the reality check we just performed and generate a list of potential measures we can track. It's in this step that the value of assessing your reality begins to pay dividends. Look at each attribute of your reality and challenge yourself to determine what you could measure in order to improve the situation. In many cases you may come up with projects rather than measures, for example, "We have no customer loyalty program, so we need to create one." That's fine. The associated measure could be "Percentage milestone completion of customer loyalty program."

Way Forward

In this, the final step, we look at our brainstormed list of potential measures and select the critical few that are most critical in our attempt to achieve the objective.

> It will help to look at the list you've created and determine whether there is a natural order to what you've documented. Are there dependencies among the measures (some have to occur before others can be undertaken)? If so, put first things first. We also suggest you think in terms of lagging and leading indicators. The lag in our example could be "market share," which at the end of the day is the ultimate arbiter of the objective. However, it should be accompanied by a leading indicator designed to move you forward on one of the key impediments identified during the reality stage. As noted above, that may be "Percentage milestone completion on the customer loyalty program."

Selecting better performance measures is one of the best things you can do to improve your performance as it provides regular insights for discussion and analysis. Follow this four-step GROW guide and you'll be well on your way.

MAKE THE TOUGH CHOICE – LIMIT YOUR MEASURES TO THOSE THAT MATTER

"We need to come up with new measures. The ones we have are trending too low."

Paul was channel surfing recently and came across the 2000 film *High Fidelity* starring John Cusack as Rob, a thirty-something record-store owner in Chicago. Rob loves compiling lists and ranking things. In fact, the movie centers around the list of his "Top 5 Breakups." He and his coworkers have spirited debates about myriad other topics as well, and it's clear they've put serious thought and consideration into their choices when stitching together personal rankings. While watching, Paul drifted back to work mode for a moment and wondered: *Do organizations put that much thought into choosing their measures of success?*

That may seem like a silly question. Of course, teams and individuals devote significant mental energy to selecting their measures. Right? Maybe not. The primary reason we suggest this is the sheer number of measures (or key results in the OKR world) attached to objectives. It's not uncommon to have six, seven, eight or more tied to a given objective. If you've done even a cursory amount of research on performance measurement, you know the importance of measuring what matters. It's all about focus — homing in on the critical elements of success.

Here are three reasons that measures accumulate, and what you can do about it.

1. *Mistaking tasks or activities for measures*

   This is something we see frequently. When crafting measures, writers will list not only the ultimate outcome; the evidence of success on the objective, but every granular step necessary to reach that outcome. To differentiate between a task and a measure, use this simple test: If you can accomplish the action in a relatively short period of time, it's more likely a task than a true measure. And if you do find yourself listing tasks, ask, "What will happen when I complete these tasks?" Doing so will lead to a quantitative measure.

2. *FOMO*

   Which stands for "fear of missing out." Broadening that just a bit, some measurement drafters simply don't want to leave anything out. They feel it's safer simply to list every possible result, regardless of whether it provides evidence of achievement of the objective or not. As noted above, focus should be your aim here, not quantity of metrics.

3. *Busy bee syndrome*

   There are those among us who will use the measurement process as a stage to demonstrate how busy they are. These martyrs will create multiple objectives, each with a mountain of measures, the totality of which quickly ascends to an impossible number of items to accomplish in the given timeframe. Always remember, measures are not meant to showcase your crushing workload or provide a glorified to-do list.

A favorite quote of ours comes from a book titled *How To Think Like Leonardo da Vinci*. And who wouldn't want to think like one of the greatest polymaths in history? The book's author Michael Gelb has this to say about the task of making difficult choices: "The discipline of ordering … the discipline of choosing one over another, ranking one a level higher than another, and then articulating why you chose the way you did requires a depth and clarity of consideration and comparison that inspires richer appreciation and enjoyment."[i] There is no better way to describe the arduous, but ultimately rewarding, process of selecting objectives and measures of genuine value. Although it's a difficult assignment, the hard work of making the demanding choices will leave you with a richer appreciation of what you do select.

Source:

[i] Michael J. Gelb, *How to Think Like Leonardo da Vinci*. New York: Bantam Dell, 2004.

THE POWER OF COUNTERBALANCED MEASURES

"Hang on, Ferguson. I need to counterbalance your boring report with some cat videos."

Whenever we create performance measures, we do so with the intention of monitoring results so that we can learn from what's happened, and hopefully improve in the future. But measurement is more than numbers. Any time you monitor something it will impact behavior, and it's important to consider those elements when creating your metrics. Here's an example from an information technology (IT) team we worked with recently.

This group was in the process of developing measures throughout their organization, taking that all-important step of using the power of linked performance metrics to generate alignment from top to bottom. At one point during the workshop, their team lead asked a question that had been bothering him.

IT Team Lead: "We've been told that minimizing expenses is crucial to the organization, and so we've created a measure of reducing vendor costs. What we're going to do is negotiate with software and hardware vendors, and consultants to try and drive down our overall IT costs."

Us: "And if you do that, what will happen?"

IT Team Lead: "Well, we're concerned that if we insist on lower costs from our vendors that could lead them to cut some corners, and ultimately result in poorer service to our customers here in the company … and that's the last thing we want to happen."

It was clear from the look on his face this was a dedicated professional who wanted to do the right thing for the organization, but was concerned that his measures could actually *harm* his goals by creating some unintended consequences. So, we recommended a counterbalanced measure to mitigate the risk.

The IT lead knew that reducing costs was important to the bottom line but didn't want those lower costs translating into poorer service for his customers. Therefore, he chose a measure of "customer satisfaction with IT services" to counterbalance vendor costs. Over time he'll monitor the two, looking for correlations that may require his intervention. If, for example, vendor costs do decrease but he also sees a decline in customer satisfaction, he can hypothesize the two are correlated and use this information to possibly reconsider targets for vendor cost reduction. Maybe the initial target was too aggressive, leading to a degradation of the services provided to his customers.

Consider these ideas as you create your own measures.

1. *Review what you have now*

   Carefully review each measure you currently track and critically examine what behaviors they may drive within (and outside) your organization.

2. *Add counterbalanced measures where applicable*

   For any measures you feel hold the potential of driving the wrong behavior, work to create a counterbalanced measure you can monitor to mitigate any negative effects.

3. *Take action*

   In the example above, the IT manager decided that monitoring customer satisfaction could counterbalance lower vendor costs. Once you see a negative reaction occurring, in this case if costs are going down (that's good) but so is satisfaction (that's bad), you need to intervene immediately. How severe is the dip in satisfaction, and what is more important — lowering your costs or keeping customers happy? That's an important strategic discussion to have, and it can only be held once you have the data to support it.

An old saying reminds us, "You get what you measure." Therefore, it's critical to think carefully about the potential ramifications of the measures you're using to run your business today, ensuring you're balancing any possible negative outcomes with measures that provide an early warning system for analysis and remediation.

TARGET REBELLION

"Yes, sir. We're hitting all Targets."

A few years back one of us (Tor Inge) encountered a peculiar situation. A CEO of an organization that Tor Inge worked with ordered his team to implement a new software solution and achieve the desired results within two weeks. The team had no clear strategy, no resources, no processes in place, no commitment from the management, and no plans for how to reach this target. *Two weeks!* thought Tor Inge. *There is no way this can be done.* The project was set to fail, and the team knew it.

"You should go back to your CEO and tell him two weeks is not feasible," Tor Inge advised the team, but they refused. As Tor Inge came to learn, the mantra of this organization was, "A target which is dictated has to be delivered." It was a matter of respect and cultural norms. Although this may seem odd, for the team to attempt to reach a target that they knew they couldn't reach was culturally more acceptable than questioning the CEO's request. Tor Inge wasn't a fan of this approach, but there was nothing he could say or do to change the team's mind.

As the project got underway, all milestones were missed, and the CEO wasn't happy. He was confused as to why things were taking so long and questioned the team's abilities. It wasn't a good situation. The team eventually managed to get the solution up and running; however, the implementation took far longer than two weeks and put everyone involved under unnecessary stress.

Target setting plays an important part in your organizational strategy. It is okay to set up ambitious targets; however, they must be realistic and accompanied by a well-defined plan on how to reach them. When unrealistic targets are set, it's crucial to speak up — raise a target rebellion! Often, CEOs might not be aware of the appropriate time, cost, and resources it takes to deliver a project and will gladly adjust their expectations to set their team up for success.

THE JOY OF SETTING TARGETS

"You really think that dressing up as Robin Hood will help us reach our targets?!"

How do you feel about setting targets? If the research is accurate, you probably fall into one of two camps. Some people are convinced that targets improve performance by sharpening focus on specific goals that truly matter. There is ample evidence to support this. In fact some researchers have suggested that goal-directed planning (setting targets) stimulates electrical activity in the frontal lobes of our brain and can increase happiness. In the opposite corner are those who believe targets are awash with issues, including stress and demotivation when set overly high, lack of guidance in what to do to achieve them, and most troubling, the possibility of ethical violations in attempts to meet them.

Neither of us is a trained academic in the science of goal-setting behavior, but between us we have over fifty combined years of experience in working with organizations around the globe. That real-world, on the ground, and in the corporate trenches time has demonstrated to us that, when established effectively and fairly, targets can without a doubt boost performance. They do so in many ways, but an emerging benefit, one that is vital in today's ultra-competitive landscape, is a compelling target's ability to motivate innovative thinking, often leading to breakthrough results.

Here are a few ideas to create better targets in your organization:

1. *Make target setting a dialogue*

   Since your subordinates are ultimately responsible for reaching their targets, they need to have a strong voice in setting them. To set targets that are fair and realistic, invite your subordinates for an open dialogue to discuss targets and measures for achieving them. Be clear and direct in your expectations, but ensure you understand your subordinates' rationale as well. You must set your perspective aside to truly hear theirs. Be actively present and challenge them to justify their thinking. Active listening and challenging questions such as "What do you need if we should set the target 20% higher?" will help keep your conversations focused and productive. When both parties feel heard and understood, you're sure to come to a mutually beneficial agreement.

2. *Don't go in blind*

   Before you set a target for anything in your business, you must develop insights on what is being measured. If, for example, you're setting a target on customer satisfaction, it's imperative that you attempt to understand what drives satisfaction for your customers. Only then can you create a meaningful target. This advice applies to targets reflecting any component of your business.

3. *Create plans for achievement*

   Related to the suggestion above, before landing on a target, carefully map out what it will take to achieve it. Consider the process changes it may require, customer analysis it necessitates, specific projects or strategic initiatives to achieve it, and so on. Determining the level of effort and resources required to meet a target will assist you in validating its appropriateness.

As Henry Royce, co-founder of the luxury carmaker Rolls Royce, noted, "Strive for perfection in everything you do. Take the best that exists and make it better. When it does not exist, design it." Challenging targets demand new ways of thinking about problems, and the solutions will often catapult you ahead of your competition.

MILESTONE PARTY

"Milestone parties are great. You get to meet everyone you've been emailing from two meters away."

Track your small wins to motivate big accomplishments.
— Teresa Amabile

Serious question. Have you ever tried to run on a treadmill? It can be quite intimidating, especially if you're not used to running at all. Many people, who try it, also find it dull and uninspiring.

Tor Inge is an experienced runner. Having grown up in Norway, he's been jogging around fjords and mountains since childhood, and lately he's been doing lots of running after his grandchildren. He's not a big fan of exercising indoors; however, during a typical Norwegian winter with freezing temperatures, snowstorms, and wind chill nearing zero, a treadmill is a good alternative to running outside.

It happened during one of those extra cold winter days when Tor Inge decided to hop on a treadmill and run a half marathon — 21 kilometers (13.1 miles). It was a spur-of-the-moment idea with no specific motive aside from giving his body some exercise. Running such a distance is a challenging endeavor even for experienced runners, but Tor Inge had a plan.

Instead of focusing on the length of the run, Tor Inge broke the journey into chunks and celebrated every kilometer he passed. Coming onto the 16th kilometer, he imagined people clapping and cheering him on from the sidelines. It might have been all in his head; however, those cheers and small celebrations along the way are what carried him across the finish line.

The same applies to businesses. Especially with big hairy audacious goals (BHAGs), a term coined by Jim Collins and Jerry Porras in their book, *Built to Last: Successful Habits of Visionary Companies*, which are not achievable without splitting them up into minor goals and setting milestones along the journey.

What we recommend is setting a milestone for every important achievement in a project. (Make sure each milestone has a fixed date and an assigned owner.) Using milestones will help you monitor the project progress, keep the project on track, and see at a glance if things start to fall behind schedule. And here comes the best advice of all — celebrate each milestone achievement! This will not only help you and your team stay motivated throughout the journey, but it will also help lift your spirit and enhance your willingness to keep going. We need to party more!

TRULY STRATEGIC INITIATIVES

"OK, let's quickly review our few key strategic initiatives."

First, let's define our terms. To us, a truly strategic initiative is a project you undertake to help ensure you meet or exceed performance targets on key performance measures you've identified as critical to strategy execution. Strategic initiatives will have a defined scope, finite duration, specific resources attached (both human and financial), and well-defined accountabilities assigned. What should be clear is that strategic initiatives aren't designed to tackle day-to-day problems (although as a side benefit, they may do that) but instead are focused on driving significant improvements in targeted strategic areas. A strategic initiative could be anything from installing a customer relationship management system to launching a new career development program for your teams.

Most organizations we work with are literally drowning in projects they consider to be strategic. After conducting an inventory throughout the company, it's not uncommon for larger firms to have a roster of a hundred or more. But are they truly strategic? Typically, the answer is no. Projects frequently spring up as a kneejerk reaction to an operational issue and ultimately take on a life of their own with little monitoring, evaluation, or demonstrated results. This takes a substantial toll on the organization in the form of wasted resources (especially time spent in endless meetings), redundant efforts, and increased costs. While no magic number of strategic initiatives exists, in our experience, even large and complex organizations should expect to be managing just a small portfolio of five to ten truly strategic initiatives. Outlined below are two "must dos" to ensure your pool of initiatives is, in fact, strategic.

1. *Map your projects to your strategic goals and objectives*

   This is the simplest and most powerful advice we can offer. Take the time and effort to critically examine each and every project in your organization, and map it back to your stated strategic goals. If a project is not serving an objective you've identified as strategic, it should be eliminated. This, however, is often easier said than done for a couple of reasons. First, many initiatives become the "pet project" of an executive who is loath to admit it isn't contributing to the organization's success. He or she may have a personal vested interest in its success and be reluctant to let it go. In this case, a strong chief executive is required to act in the best interests of the firm, despite any hard feelings that may engender. Second, many organizations will fall prey to the "sunk cost fallacy," believing that although the project has yet to produce strategic benefits, they've invested significant resources already and that investment justifies future commitment to the project.

2. *Track initiatives thoroughly*

   The global consulting firm McKinsey has reported that just over half of the organizations they surveyed track execution of their strategic initiatives. This is one of those head-shaking statistics that makes you want to scream, "*What!*" Given this evidence, there is little wonder that many projects run amok, racking up precious resources in the form of time and money, when nobody is watching. A vast body of easily accessible literature exists on project management, and step two for any strategic initiative should be adhering to the basics of sound project management (scope, resources, accountabilities, expected return on investment, milestones, etc.). Additionally, strategic initiative progress should be a standing item on senior executive business performance reviews.

It's not uncommon to discover that you simultaneously have too many and too few strategic initiatives. Many organizations will have a multitude of projects that don't meaningfully contribute to strategic aims, and too few that actually do move the needle on execution. Follow the steps above to ensure your time, energy, and precious resources are dedicated to the initiatives that really matter.

MY KEY RESULT OR MEASURE IS NOT NECESSARILY YOUR OBJECTIVE

"The only OKR that you need to worry about is making me look good!"

One of us (Paul) spent some time early in his career working in public accounting. No offense to accountants everywhere, but it wasn't his favorite time, and he's long since retired his calculator. However, one of the comforting aspects of that occupation was the knowledge that no matter how challenging or esoteric a problem he faced, he knew there was an answer in the form of "generally accepted accounting principles," or GAAP, the set of rules guiding all accounting actions and decisions. In the OKR and Balanced Scorecard worlds, we don't have any such guiding principles, but some "rules" have surfaced that seem to be unbreakable, among them in some quarters, the fact that when you (the boss) create a key result (measure in the Balanced Scorecard system), that becomes my (the employee) objective. This is as pure a definition of the old cascading model as possible, and the fact is, it's not correct and can be damaging to your strategy execution effort.

There are at least two reasons this is the case. Note that for simplicity below, we'll use OKR language, but everything stated applies to the Balanced Scorecard as well.

1. *It's simply not practical*

   Unless you're working in sales, perhaps the only function in which a pure cascading model may prove applicable, your key result may not be a direct fit for my role, function, or responsibilities in a way that makes it possible for me to effectively execute it at my level. It's akin to the old "square peg in a round hole" challenge. I may adopt your key result as my objective, but in reality there is little I can do to influence or execute it, and thus the OKR I create, while technically aligned, proves irrelevant and unlikely to motivate performance.

2. *It robs people of intrinsic motivation*

Mountains of research point to the power of intrinsic motivation — engaging in an activity because we're internally motivated to do so, rather than being induced to do so with some form of external reward (extrinsic motivation). What's even more compelling is that intrinsic motivation can enhance creative results, and that's exactly what we're after when drafting OKRs — visionary and innovative ways of executing our strategy. In one interesting experiment that demonstrates the point convincingly, creative writers wrote poems on the topic of snow.[i] Then, one-third of the writers was assigned (without their knowledge) to an extrinsic motivation group. They were given a short "Reasons for Writing" questionnaire that asked them to consider reasons for being a writer; all of the items, according to previous research, were extrinsic. For example, being financially secure from writing a successful novel. A second group also filled out a questionnaire that had only intrinsic reasons, such as "the opportunity for self-expression." The final third of writers (control group) spent a few minutes reading an irrelevant story. Then the writers wrote a second poem on laughter. At this point all of the poems were judged for creativity. The results were clear. Although the pre-measure poems (on snow) displayed no differences, those on the topic of laughter written by the group who had contemplated extrinsic motivation were significantly lower in creativity from the others. Just five minutes spent thinking about extrinsic rewards had lowered their intrinsic motivation, and hence creativity.

This is the substantial risk we take when forcing our OKRs on teams below us. In effect we're saying, "*Make this your objective because I said so.*" It is the ultimate expression of extrinsic motivation, which strips away any opportunity for them to creatively engage with the OKR above them and determine a compelling OKR that signals their direct contribution to success. Rather than cascading OKRs, we should focus on connecting. Share your OKR with the team below you, explain your rationale for selecting it, and engage in a conversation with the team on how they might influence it at their level. This approach will facilitate alignment to overall strategic direction but allow for local variations and interpretations that drive creative expression and more meaningful OKRs at all levels.

Source:

[i] Teresa Amabile and Steven Kramer, *The Progress Principle: Using Small Wins to Ignite Joy, Engagement, and Creativity at Work.*

BEWARE THE SILVER LINING REPORTS

"On a positive note, the weather will be nice next week."

Nobody cares how much you know,
until they know how much you care.
— Theodore Roosevelt

If you follow politics, you know the drill of political campaigns leading up to an election. Catchy slogans, theme songs, social media ads, speeches, influencers, exhaustive reports, and other means are used in an effort to sway voters in the party's favor. What's interesting, however, is the post-election period.

No matter the outcome, after an election takes place, all parties tend to celebrate and emphasize the silver lining. You'll often hear statements such as ("We didn't win, but ...") "we improved compared to the last poll," "we performed better than we did last election," "we gained more votes in the western part of the country than last year," "we are the winners!"

At times you can observe a similar notion in business. Many managers are too ashamed of reporting losses so they will overstate positive results on less significant metrics — "We saved $200 on office supplies this month!" — and play down negative results on important metrics — "We had to close down our Milwaukee office." To prevent these silver lining reports, make sure to encourage trust and transparency in your organization. When the numbers yield negative results, report it, cut your losses, and move on.

Here are three tips for building and cultivating trust in your organization.

1. *Walk the talk*

   Building trust in the workplace starts with you. If you expect your employees to be transparent with you, you must be transparent with them. Keep your promises, ensure everyone is informed about your organization's performance, and always align your behavior with the organization's values.

2. *Give praise when it's due*

   Acknowledge good performance and give praise when it's due. Employees who receive recognition from their leaders are more likely to trust them. Be transparent about your and your organization's wins and (especially) failures to encourage transparent communication across your organization.

3. *Be honest and supportive*

   Show support to your employees even when mistakes are made. Being honest, setting expectations, and providing feedback for a job well done (or not-so-well done) are all forms of transparency that build trust. Don't ever punish your employees for reporting "bad news."

MORE DATA ≠ MORE BUSINESS SUCCESS

"Are we successful yet?"

Recently one of us (Tor Inge) was speaking at a Business Intelligence conference in Germany. It was a big event with hundreds of vendors and thousands of attendees. What became apparent after sitting through several keynotes is that most presenters considered data to be the "holy grail" of business success. "The knowledge and power are in the data," read one of the slides. As a strategy execution advocate, Tor Inge presented a different view.

He opened his presentation by sharing an insight from a book called *Good to Great: Why Some Companies Make the Leap ... and Others Don't* written by Jim Collins. When Collins researched what made some companies "world-class," he learned the following:

> *We found no evidence that good-to-great companies had more or better information than the comparison companies. None.*

The room fell silent. It was at that moment when Tor Inge felt as if everyone in the room was about to throw their hefty conference binders at him. How dare he question the importance of data! Please don't misunderstand us; collecting data is essential for any organization. It is the means of measuring performance and making informed decisions. The point that Tor Inge was trying to make is that more data does not equal more business success.

more data ≠ more business success

With that in mind, allow us to adjust the statement from the conference slide: "There is knowledge in the data, the power is in what you do with it." Most business intelligence

(BI) tools are built to collect data; however, they fall short in putting your data to work. If you're looking to use your data in a way that drives your business forward, a business management software will be a better choice for you.

USING INDIVIDUAL GOALS IN TIMES OF CRISIS

"I know we said Aloha Friday, Gilbert, but wearing a coconut bra might be taking it a bit too far."

September 11, 2001, represented a crisis. The global financial meltdown of 2008 was a crisis. However, as we write this book mid-2020, we're experiencing perhaps the greatest economic shock/crisis ever unleashed on the world: the global COVID-19 pandemic. The spread of the novel coronavirus has forced many millions to shelter in place and perform their jobs from home, as workplaces around the world shut their doors. This mass migration of workers from offices back to their homes brings with it many challenges: balancing work and pressing family demands, avoiding the temptation to work constantly even if just for the sake of distraction, and missing the social element provided by our "normal" work environments, to name just a few. We believe individual level employee goals are crucial in times of great crisis such as COVID-19 or whatever we may face in the future. Outlined below are our reasons for suggesting this.

1. *Individual goals provide a link back to purpose and strategy*

   When we're isolated from our normal working environment, it's easy to quickly lose perspective on what's strategically important to the overall organization. Lacking the regular cadence of team meetings on priorities and spontaneous hallway chats with coworkers on business issues, we may adopt tunnel vision on simple tasks and lose sight of what matters most. Assigning individual goals provides a mechanism for managers to ensure the strategy and purpose link is maintained as workers are unmoored from their normal circumstances. Before assigning the task to an individual employee of creating a goal, a manager must first outline the business's current priorities, and it's likely these have changed dramatically in light of a crisis. This conversation ensures there is understanding at the team member level of what is at stake and how their personal contribution is necessary to help the entire organization work through its present challenges.

2. *Emotional support is provided*

   In times of crisis, we want to know that our leaders, both political and organizational, have our back and are in our corner. Setting goals offers a forum for leaders to provide the emotional support many employees are craving. We recommend that managers check in with their employees once a week on the individual's goals. That may place an administrative burden on the manager in the short term, but the benefits far outweigh the bureaucratic cost. During these check-ins, leaders have the opportunity to go well beyond an evaluation of their charge's goals, and can provide much-needed support. Employees working from home may feel confused and isolated, and these conversations can allay some of those issues as managers share their own concerns, stories, and coping mechanisms. Empathy can be a powerful tool in a time of crisis.

3. *Goals ensure focus is maintained*

   When disconnected from our office routines, it can be difficult to determine what we should be working on in order to continue creating value for the organization. Answering emails, hanging out on company slack channels, and keeping up to date on social media can easily fill the day, but in the end, is that the best use of our time? By asking individuals to create goals, you're challenging them to determine, even in times of relative chaos, the most strategic actions they can take. If you're a manager, and assuming you've followed the advice already provided, you'll also use the opportunity to lend much need emotional support to team members and provide detailed updates on the company's priorities.

The jury remains out, and likely will for some time, on whether individual-level goals are right for every organization. However, times of crisis represent uncharted territory and we need all the help we can get navigating an unfamiliar and unsettling landscape. Individual goals can help bring a welcome and comforting source of the "normal" in what is decidedly an abnormal time.

GOVERNANCE

WHAT COMES FIRST – GOVERNANCE OR CULTURE?

There is nothing more difficult to take in hand, more perilous to conduct, or more uncertain in its success than to take the lead in the introduction of a new order of things.

— Niccolò Machiavelli

We've been doing this work for many years and thought we had heard just about every possible question related to strategy and strategy execution, until, that is, we got this query at a recent event: "When you develop a Balanced Scorecard, what's more important, putting in a governance system or ingraining it in the culture?" For those of you who don't have a Balanced Scorecard, it could be any type of new system — OKR, the 4 Disciplines of Execution, anything. Out of the gate, do you focus on creating a governance system or attempt to make it part of your cultural landscape? Obviously, for any new execution system to demonstrate results over the long haul, both of these conditions are necessary. However, we do feel there is a logical order: First comes governance, then follows culture.

Let's assume your organization has adopted OKR, and it's the first time you've instituted the framework. Job one will be convincing people (executives, managers, and employees alike) to actually use the system. We've both witnessed companies that create outstanding OKR programs that hold the potential to provide tremendous value, but literally wither on the vine from lack of use. Human nature is such that folks will always gravitate toward the status quo, which in this case translates to ignoring the new system hoping it will go away. Therefore, you need to institute systems and processes to lay a solid foundation for your new OKR program.

The best way to do this is to make it easy for people to use the tool. Change is most likely to happen when it represents the path of least resistance. There's a reason that even as we age, many of our closest friends are those we grew up with; they lived close by, making interactions easy. When it comes to a new OKR program (for example), we can make things easier by scheduling regular review meetings in advance, and making them sacrosanct on calendars. A software system can be used to collect data, eliminating the time-consuming and cumbersome effort required by manual collection. Also, someone can be elected to facilitate initial review meetings, setting the agenda, teeing up questions, documenting action items, and so on. By putting in place a few simple rules that make it easy for people to use the system, the probability of uptake is enhanced significantly.

As you launch any type of change initiative, ask yourself these questions:

1. *Is the purpose of the change clear?*

   For employees to accept any change they must first fully understand why you're undertaking it in the first place. Be sure to ceaselessly communicate the rationale of your change before going into launch mode.

2. *Have we made it easy for people to use the new system?*

   People are stubborn in their refusal to change, so have them literally trip over the new tool with rules and processes that facilitate initial use.

3. *How can we make this new framework part of our culture?*

   Cultural change doesn't come quickly. However, that doesn't preclude you from thinking of and testing ways you might insert the new system into your culture.

As your implementation matures, you can segue to ingraining the new program into the cultural fabric of your organization. Cultures are slow to change and evolve, but there are things you can do to accelerate the process. For example, rename the system to something that is more culturally relevant to your organization, one that befits your reason for engaging with the framework. The simple act of naming something tends to personalize it, replacing sterile corporate-speak with a meaningful and aspirational moniker. If you hope to achieve moonshot-type results with your new change program, start with governance and cultural change will follow.

THE SECRET INGREDIENT TO STRATEGY EXECUTION SUCCESS... HINT: IT'S GOVERNANCE

"They say that good governance is like a recipe, so we invited an expert."

As we write this, objectives and key results (OKR) are definitely enjoying a moment. Popularity is sky-high, with implementation numbers soaring globally, and no wonder. When applied with rigor and discipline, OKR can deliver enhanced focus, alignment, employee engagement, and numerous other benefits. It's that pesky "rigor and discipline" phrase we'd like to acknowledge and explore here. And by the way, this applies to any strategy execution effort, be it OKR, Balanced Scorecard, 4DX, and so on. Three of the most sought-after benefits of any execution initiative are accountability, alignment, and focus. Let's examine each through the lens of governance.

1. *Negotiate and analyze to drive accountability*

   Let's say you decide to implement OKR at the team level. All teams now have objectives and key results. This step alone will not boost accountability. It has to be accompanied by at least a two-step process. Step one is the approval of OKRs. Each team must draft OKRs, then enter into a negotiation with their boss to ensure both strategic alignment with company goals, and shared understanding as to the desired business impact of the OKRs. Come the end of the quarter, it's time for step two: Each team needs to meet once again with their leader, this time to review and analyze results. What happened, why did it happen, what are we going to do about what we learned? Accountability stems from the discussion of OKRs at both the time of creation, and more importantly, at the time of review.

2. *Highlight dependencies to increase alignment*

   Unfortunately, instituting OKR doesn't magically eliminate silos and promote cross-functional collaboration. OKRs can help with this, but only if you put in place the mechanisms for real conversations to take place on dependencies and shared OKRs. When crafting OKRs, each team should document who they rely on for assistance and carefully and specifically — not using bland generalities — document exactly what they need, whether it's in the form of engineering hours, marketing expertise, accounting advice, and so on. Saying "We need marketing's help on this" does nothing to solve your alignment problem. Articulating dependencies is the easy part. Now you must find the discipline to ensure teams with dependencies hold face-to-face meetings to discuss what is required from each, should they hope to achieve their OKRs. And, building on that, you'll require another layer of governance to discuss escalations for the inevitable circumstance of teams not agreeing on levels of support.

3. *Engage in disciplined thinking to enhance focus*

   All strategy execution systems are designed to help you focus on what matters most, but we have seen many organizations do the opposite. Rather than engage in the mentally taxing effort of methodical thinking about what is most vital, they do the opposite and litter their roster of OKRs with anything that could possibly impact success. Governance in this case takes the form of disciplined strategic thought when contemplating and drafting OKRs. There is likely an inverse relationship between the amount of time taken to draft an OKR, and its effectiveness as a driver of execution. Those that are thrown together quickly tend to feature generic phrases such as "increase efficiency," and "improve quality." Vague words that are open to interpretation will not drive the clarity and focus promised by OKRs.

Nothing documented here is necessarily difficult. There may be logistical challenges to overcome, and habits to form, but at the end of the day, should you hope to get the most from your investment in strategy execution, what it truly requires is a commitment to put in place the machinery of good governance.

DOCUMENT JUNGLE

"The CEO wants our department to be less of a jungle, so we're getting rid of all plants."

For every minute spent in organizing, an hour is earned.
— Benjamin Franklin

One of Tor Inge's recent consulting endeavors was helping a large government organization develop a better governance framework and reach company-wide strategic alignment. The project started with a general audit to assess what processes were currently being used and determine where the gaps were. Right off the bat, Tor Inge ran into a roadblock.

There were dozens of documents to review! There were strategic plans, strategic roadmaps, strategic initiatives, department action plans, KPI justifications, SWOT analyses, business objectives assessments, and all sorts of other documents, some of which dated back to the '90s! Some were buried deep in folders on the company's server, some were posted in a hallway on a bulletin board, and some lived in dusty binders. It was a jungle! What's worse, each document was structured a little differently and told a slightly different story. There was a lot of duplication, redundancy, and, in some cases, contradiction. No wonder everyone was confused!

It took several weeks of internal discussions to cut through the jungle, but the result was well worth the time. In the end the organization managed to get rid of all clutter and got on the same page in terms of strategy and plans for how to better run their internal processes. The true test of successful governance implementation, however, will be whether the organization manages to keep it up. Only time will tell.

While setting up an efficient governance framework is a complex endeavor, here are three tips that will set you on a path to good governance right away.

1. *Establish a common taxonomy*

   There is often confusion when a company lacks a set way of organizing data and files. Establishing a common taxonomy helps to prevent confusion as it provides a logical structure for organizing information, and therefore makes it easier to locate and use the information. To create a common taxonomy, decide on a logical way to structure your data and files into categories and subcategories using terminology that is easily understood by everyone in your organization. You don't need to invent new words! Tap into your departments. Chances are that your teams have already developed a list of acronyms and abbreviations for terms they frequently use. Be sure to incorporate these terms when you create your taxonomy and use them consistently when developing new documents.

2. *Create a process for information distribution*

   Develop a formal process for how to communicate your strategy and plans. Be sure to focus not only on how to distribute information from the top level down the stream throughout the organization, but also on how to transmit information back up the stream. Having a formal process in place and following this process helps to ensure that everyone in your organization feels connected to the company's strategy and direction.

3. *Business software*

   To instill good governance in your organization, you need to keep your employees informed about what is happening. In today's digital age, one of the most efficient ways to distribute information in a safe and efficient manner is through business software. A good business software tool will not only allow you to share information, but it will also enable you and your employees to ensure that processes are being followed, access documents, monitor KPIs, manage projects, set up alerts, generate reports, and operate as a unified business unit — all in all, manage your business.

KPI GRAVEYARD

One of the questions we frequently hear when consulting with different companies is how to connect their performance management system with the company's overall strategy. In a good-case scenario, the performance management system is some sort of KPI software. In a bad-case scenario, the system is a series of calendar reminders, KPI spreadsheets, and a bunch of reports jammed in a dusty filing cabinet, but that's another story. Typically, the organization has been using the system for years, and the leadership is very proud of it.

The first challenge then becomes how to convince the leadership to set their beloved system aside for a moment and shift their focus from KPIs to strategy. This process of "emptying your brain" of your cherished KPIs is hard for many. The underlying issue here is that oftentimes the leadership wants to change without having to change *their* way of doing things too much. Changing people's mindset and habits is one of the toughest things to accomplish in an organization.

The next challenge is going through the following exercise:

Step 1 – Show me your strategy

> In order to have your performance management system reflect strategy, you must first have a strategy to implement. This involves formulation of your organization's mission, vision, goals, objectives, and action plans to reach those goals and objectives.

Step 2 – Translate and structure your strategy

- Clarify your strategic objectives — what do you want to achieve?
- Show how your strategic objectives are aligned with the overall strategy — perhaps through a strategy map
- Develop a plan of how to achieve your company's objectives through establishing/aligning your company's initiatives

Step 3 – Assess your KPIs

On completing steps one and two above, look at the KPIs in your performance management system to assess which ones can function as an expression of a strategic objective achievement. Those are the KPIs you want to focus on!

Completing this exercise requires a lot of thought and all hands all deck. Don't try to do it overnight and get buy-in from the whole organization! What you're likely to realize after completing all steps is that, in terms of reaching your strategic objectives, some KPIs carry more weight than others, and that some carry no weight at all! They've been just clutter all along.

Your strategic objectives will serve as a guide on which KPIs to keep, and which ones to get rid of. It's possible that some of the KPIs that are irrelevant to your strategic objectives still represent important information, so you may want to keep those. As far as the rest is concerned, it's best to send them to the KPI graveyard.

WHY YOU MUST FRAME PERFORMANCE MEASUREMENT AS A LEARNING OPPORTUNITY

"Ah, that's not art. That's our learning curve."

Learning never exhausts the mind.

— Leonardo da Vinci

When discussing performance measurement with organizations, whether OKR or Balanced Scorecard, we emphasize the essential role of learning — what the results tell you and how you can use that information to improve performance in the future. Most people nod encouragingly, but there are inevitably a few eye rolls from the more alpha types who are saying to themselves, "Learning is great, sure, but I want to hit my numbers every time!"

There is nothing wrong with a desire to excel and achieve breakthrough performance, in fact promoting visionary thinking is one of the primary attributes and benefits of measuring strategy execution. But how you go about it matters. Framing the journey as a learning experience will prove much more beneficial than demanding results at all costs. Here are three things to consider as you frame your measurement initiative in the hearts and minds of your employees.

1. *Reinforce the focus on learning*

   Here's a very interesting experiment: University students were given three rounds of anagrams to solve. An anagram is a word or phrase created by rearranging the letters of another word. For example, listen can be reorganized as silent. In the final round of the challenge, the participants were not required to show their solutions to researchers, but merely had to check a box next to each anagram they had unscrambled. One group of students was told that the task was intended to evaluate their performance, a so-called "outcome" goal. Another group was informed that the purpose of the task was to develop their skills, a "learning" goal. The results were illuminating: 61 percent of those with an outcome goal inflated their results, versus 44 percent of those with a learning goal. The researchers suggest this result stems from the fact that outcome goals stimulate a prevention focus: People are so concerned with preventing a negative consequence that they will go to extremes to avoid falling short.[i] We don't want people inflating the results of their performance measures, so stress the learning component throughout the process.

2. *It's about getting better*

In her practical and informative book *Succeed*, author Heidi Grant Halvorson provides additional evidence of the power of framing. Her terminology differs slightly — rather than outcome versus learning goals, she uses "get better" versus "be good" goals — but the findings are strikingly similar. People who pursue goals to get better, in other words learn rather than focus on an end outcome, consistently achieve more. What is most encouraging for those of us interested in performance measurement is that as goals become more difficult and complex, a "get better" mindset seems to provide immunity to the challenge and, in fact, promotes grit and perseverance leading to sustained effort and performance. The opposite is true of "be good" goals.

3. *Try it in your own life*

Here's an example of these concepts in action from Paul. Recently I became interested in performance driving. I joined a local club and regularly participate in autocross events. An autocross is a timed competition in which drivers navigate a defined course, typically consisting of a number of tight turns and short straights. At first, my goal was purely to "be good" in nature. I wanted to be among the

> best drivers in the club and set my sights on finishing within three seconds of the day's top time. Unfortunately, my obsession with time did little to help me and left me frustrated after each event as I looked at the final timesheet and found my name mid-pack or below, always more than three seconds behind the leaders. Finally, I was able to change my approach to a focus on "getting better." That led to a greater emphasis on learning from what the data was telling me and a realization that, despite setbacks, I could continue to get better over time. That's when my times began to improve.

When launching a measurement program, be sure to follow this tested advice. Stress to everyone in your organization measuring strategy execution to never stop learning.

Source:

[i] The study was reported in "How to Set Goals that Lessen the Temptation to Cheat," *Harvard Business Review*, September–October 2019.

GETTING YOUR BOARD ON BOARD

"I got my responses ready."

Not long ago, one of us (Paul) was working with a client, helping them develop a strategy execution system, and he recommended involving the company's board of directors in the process. Since monitoring corporate performance is one of their key fiduciary responsibilities, it seemed like a good idea. As a first step, Paul suggested a short training session on the principles of strategy execution, focusing primarily on the necessity of quality metrics for gauging execution. The CEO hesitated and then said, somewhat sheepishly, "I don't think that's a good idea. They may think that (training) is beneath them." Paul protested, but ultimately the idea was scrapped.

On other occasions, we've worked with organizations whose boards, while not submitting to the indignities of training, have allowed their executives to review key performance measures with them. For the most part they sit, bored, nodding their heads occasionally, maybe asking a rote question to appear engaged, but seem perfectly content to move on to the next item of business.

We feel this sort of behavior is an enormous lost opportunity. Consider the principal obligations of a corporate board: to approve and monitor strategy, approve major financial decisions, select and evaluate executives, counsel the CEO, and of course ensure compliance with applicable laws and regulations. How can any board be expected to carry out these tasks without insight into the value-creating mechanisms of the organization, and the key metrics used to track execution? The answer — they can't. Little wonder that a full two decades after the Enron debacle we're still witnessing issues of board negligence. Referencing such calamities, Jay Lorsch, a governance expert who teaches at Harvard University, has suggested that regardless of who is responsible for epic failures such as at Enron and WorldCom, the events clearly reveal that boards need well-organized and accurate information in order to be effective. Metrics from a Balanced Scorecard or OKR can do just that.

Here are three ways to get your board on board with strategy execution.

1. *Educate them*

   Even if your board is comprised of highly accomplished and esteemed figures, chances are most of them will not be familiar with the finer points and subtleties of strategy execution techniques such as objectives and key results (OKR) or the Balanced Scorecard. Frame the education as an opportunity for them to fulfill their responsibilities by harnessing the power of proven systems, giving them additional insights into how the organization plans to demonstrate its strategic differentiation.

2. *Involve them in the process*

   As you develop your key objectives and metrics, share them with your directors, soliciting their feedback along the way. This ensures they are engaged from the outset, and you enjoy the benefits of their wisdom throughout the process. After all, your board most likely represents decades of collective knowledge that you can tap into when making decisions on how best to measure your success.

3. *Have the board develop their own measures of success*

   Challenge your directors to create performance measures that gauge their collective success. The chosen metrics could range from improving their own skills and knowledge of the company and industry to monitoring ethical or governance-related violations to monitoring executive succession.

The global consulting firm McKinsey once reported that 44 percent of directors do not fully understand the key drivers of value for the organizations they govern; and 43 percent cannot identify the key risks facing the company. Involving them in the strategy execution process from the outset can go a long way to remedying that deficiency.

Source:

For the statistic on BOD understanding of value drivers: McKinsey April–May 2002 US Directors' Survey.

IT'S TIME TO RETIRE THE TRADITIONAL PERFORMANCE REVIEW

"In the spirit of innovation, we simplified our performance review to emojis."

If you are building a culture where honest expectations are communicated and peer accountability is the norm, then the group will address poor performance and attitudes.

— Henry Cloud

Do you drive an Edsel? When you get home after a long day at work, do you sometimes have to adjust the antenna on your roof before you can enjoy one of the three channels on your black and white TV? Are your kids fighting over the family hula hoop? We doubt very much that you do any of those things, all hallmarks of the 1950s. But, the odds are very good that your company *is* doing one thing today the same way they did sixty years ago — conducting performance reviews. For the vast majority of organizations, the annual performance review process is still an archaic, painful, time-consuming, and ultimately ineffective process during which a supervisor and employee struggle through assigning grades on a fixed rating scale.

The process is fraught with problems and inefficiencies. First there is the sheer time commitment. Companies spend untold hours on reviews (Deloitte estimated the task consumed about two million hours of firm time a year); despite that fact that almost 60 percent of managers say it's ineffective. There is also the problem of biases, from both the supervisor and employee side, that leads to confusion and frustration. Finally, we must recognize that traditional reviews focus on goals set solely in the past which, because of the rapid pace of change, may be largely irrelevant when review time comes along. Try these tips to breathe new life into your performance review process.

1. *Consider something new*

   The aforementioned Deloitte is just one of a fast-growing cadre of high-profile companies abandoning the antiquated review for novel methods of assessing employee performance. "Ratingless" reviews, which are basically what you'd surmise from that title — more discussions than critical assessments — are one growing method. Others are turning to the crowd, using 360-degree feedback to help employees adapt, acquire new skills, and cope effectively with change.

2. *Introduce more frequent feedback*

   One very positive development is the change taking place in many leading organizations from out-of-date, end-of-year performance reviews to real-time tracking, coaching, and mentoring that seeks to constantly shape an employee's development. Instead of heaping praise or criticism in one bureaucratic serving at year-end, organizations encourage regular feedback, facilitating an ongoing dialog designed to enhance skill development and minimize the risks associated with festering poor performance.

3. *Ensure you understand the purpose of the review*

   In one study of performance reviews, 66 percent of respondents stated that the main purpose of the process is to decide on incentive compensation. A much smaller percentage suggested talent management as the primary goal. As Stephen Covey once admonished, "You don't mess with people's rice bowl." Conflating talent management and incentive compensation, attempting to analyze one to inform the other is a recipe for confusion, skepticism, and resentment. Ensure the aims of your review process are clear to both the evaluator and the employee.

In his 2015 book, *Work Rules*, Laszlo Bock, the former Senior Vice President of People Operations at Google, has this to say about performance reviews: "Performance management as practiced by most organizations has become a rule-based bureaucratic process, existing as an end in itself rather than actually shaping performance. Employees hate it. Managers hate it. Even HR departments hate it." It doesn't have to be that way, however. By following the tips above, and maintaining a commitment to new and novel approaches to performance reviews, you can implement a process that works for everyone.

Sources:

The statistics on the effectiveness and purpose of performance reviews were drawn from http://blog.impraise.com/360-feedback/deloitte-joins-adobe-and-accenture-in-dumping-performance-reviews-360-feedback on May 2, 2016

CREATE MORE ALIGNMENT BY FOCUSING ON THE TRUE MEANING OF COMMITMENT

"Our waterfall of cascading goals is crucial to our success!"

Ask any CEO if they value the concept of alignment and they'll be spouting its virtues before you finish the question. But true top-to-bottom alignment — that rarified state characterized by an organization whose employees (all of them) understand the strategy and how they uniquely contribute to its successful execution — is unicorn rare. In an attempt to create it, many companies turn to the concept of cascaded goals: Start at the top and have goals flow down throughout the organization in a manner that allows teams at every level to track their own aligned and meaningful metrics. As part of this conversation, you'll often hear leaders espousing the value of having teams "commit to their goals."

In many cases, however, it's virtually impossible for employees to commit to goals because of the method of cascading that is applied. In a disturbingly large number of companies, despite emerging neuroscience and years of evidence, senior management still rely on the old model of forcing goals — those they believe will have the greatest impact on execution — down to lower levels, with no room for negotiation or compromise. Lip service may be paid to involving everyone in setting goals across the company, but when push comes to shove it's the senior leadership team that is dictating what is tracked at each and every level, month in and month out.

This antiquated approach is doomed for a number of reasons, but let's focus on just one, represented by a single word that was introduced in the first paragraph: commit. This verb, which can be traced to the late fourteenth century, comes from the Latin "*committere,*" meaning "to entrust, unite, combine, or bring together." When, as a senior manager, you push goals down to the next level, inhibiting any discussion or room for individual adjustments, the last thing you're doing is entrusting, uniting, combining, or bringing together. Actually, the opposite is true. You're showing a complete lack of trust in the judgment of your teams, which will inevitably sow seeds of skepticism and hamper initiative in reaching the goals you alone consider worth pursuing. After all, who is going to commit to something they had no part in creating?

If you want true commitment, try this:

1. *Foster a meaningful dialog with your teams*

   Allow them to thoughtfully consider and recommend the objectives they feel maximize their impact and have the greatest effect on overall company execution. When you do so, you are in fact entrusting, uniting, combining, and bringing together. Additionally, this simple and pragmatic process enables your team to create an emotional attachment to the goals, since they themselves were responsible for their creation.

2. *Allow room for negotiation in the process*

   You should strive to engage your teams in a spirited discussion and negotiation. It's not a matter of one side winning or losing. It's about finding the right objectives for all teams and individuals, those that facilitate alignment from top to bottom and accelerate your execution.

3. *Be open to new ideas*

   One of the biases that hampers effective performance measurement is a fixation on the status quo. In other words, it's always easier to measure what you've always measured. However, it's often the new and missing measures that drive the greatest value in advancing your strategic agenda. Give your teams the latitude to imagine the metrics that truly matter to them, even if some of them are entirely new.

The legendary American football coach Vince Lombardi once remarked, "Individual commitment to a group effort — that is what makes a team work, a company work, a society work, a civilization work." When the time comes to align goals from top to bottom, ensuring your team or organization "works," start by adhering to the true meaning of commitment.

PUNISHMENT OR REWARD

"Yes, yes, reward them. Reward them with more work."

People work for money but go the extra mile
for recognition, praise and rewards.
— Dale Carnegie

Many companies are using their performance management system for controlling and punishing teams that are not meeting their targets. It's seldom we hear about companies rewarding teams for good results. And that's a shame! We need to celebrate more.

Having a formal or informal employee reward system in place as a part of your organizational governance is a great way to motivate employees individually or in a group. It's about noticing the small wins, highlighting them, showing gratitude, and celebrating together as a team. A reward in a form of quick celebration helps employees know that their contributions are valued and appreciated, and it encourages them to do their best work.

Taking time to celebrate your teams' wins might seem like extra effort; however, trust us when we say that a little praise can go a long way. Improved company culture, enhanced team effort, and increased productivity are just some of the outcomes to expect when your employees feel valued. Short on resources? No problem. You don't have to overthink this!

While monetary rewards are always welcome, your reward system might simply consist of an impromptu cake get-together, ordering a surprise breakfast, or taking your team to a happy hour. Perhaps you introduce a gong or some other musical instrument in your office that is used to signal celebration for winning a new deal. You decide the rules!

It can be as simple as this: Target achieved > Send email to the local baker and order a cake for delivery > Send out an invitation to the people responsible for the target achievement > Celebrate!

Be fair and genuine, and keep your celebrations fun and light. (Nothing will annoy your staff more than a forced cheer in a group setting.) When employees feel sincerely appreciated by their leadership, it incentivizes them to continue contributing and excelling. Moreover, it increases their job satisfaction and happiness levels, and happy employees produce the best work.

WANT MORE SHARING AND TRANSPARENCY? START WITH BETTER MEETINGS

"Once again, our #1 OKR for the next quarter is to stay awake during our meetings."

Those who know WHAT they do tend to work harder.
Those who know WHY tend to work smarter.
— Simon Sinek

Most organizations pursuing a measurement and strategy execution system such as the Balanced Scorecard or OKR will opt for open communication of all goals, throughout the company. They're striving for transparency, which fosters shared understanding of goals and promotes cross-functional collaboration as teams recognize opportunities for cooperation.

Transparency often begins at a quarterly town hall meeting or another gathering of multiple groups, during which each team or department outlines the goals they've chosen for the upcoming period. While the range of effectiveness of these meetings varies widely, many organizations struggle to maintain a productive level of dialog and discussion. By the latter part of the meeting, the session often devolves into a rapid-fire reading of goals with absolutely no questions or requests for clarifications arising from an often bored and otherwise engaged (with their phones and laptops) audience stooped in their chairs stealing glances at the clock.

Here are three ideas to assist you in harnessing the power of transparency through better engagement of your meeting participants.

1. *Remember the story*

   Every story ever told — your favorite novel, movie, or play — adheres to a roughly similar formula. It starts with conflict, the problem faced by the protagonist compelling him or her to action. Next comes transition, the phase of the story during which our hero ventures forth into the world encountering increasingly difficult obstacles on their chosen path. Every story reaches a climactic point of action or drama during which the protagonist either achieves, or is denied, their ultimate quest. Finally, the story closes with the "new normal" state for our hero. The problem in most goal sharing meetings is that virtually all groups will simply read aloud their goals. In our schema above, that's the climax of the story. But without the conflict and transition we, the audience, have no context for that climax. Little wonder we don't engage — we don't know what led the group to that choice of goals. Imagine how much more impactful a presentation would be if a group began by outlining the specific challenges they face at this moment, the conflict in their environment. Then they pivot to discuss the options they considered to overcome those challenges in the form of goals (their transition). Now we're ready to hear the selected goals; we have the context necessary to either agree or challenge their choice. The takeaway here is this: Don't allow your groups to simply read what is on the screen behind them. Challenge them to frame their goals in a story. It's better for them, and much better for engaging the audience.

2. *Draw on the wisdom of Steven Covey*

One of our favorite (of many) principles put forth by the management guru Steven Covey is "Three-Person Teaching." Covey rightly believed that the best way to learn anything is to teach it. We can draw on that wisdom to improve the engagement in our goal sharing meetings. Before the meeting assign dis-similar groups to conduct the initial presentation of another team's goals. Perhaps HR will be assigned to present the engineering department's goals and vice versa. The team who owns the goal will of course embellish the presentation with additional details, and answer any questions, but this process forces teams to learn more about other functions work, building empathy and laying the path for potential collaboration. Each period you can reshuffle the deck, building bridges between what could previously be considered unrelated functions.

3. *Use theme teams*

    In this approach you nominate teams or individuals to provide summaries of presented goals and begin the discussion period. One option is to make three teams (this is an arbitrary number) the official observers for the first set of presentations. Make it clear that it will be incumbent on them to offer their feedback at the conclusion of the first round of goals. Of course, others may chime in as well, but at the very least you've guaranteed the attention of a subset of your audience. A second option is to draw randomly from the group — after a set of presentations, choose a random set of teams to offer input. This forces everyone in the room to stay present.

Measurement systems require disciplined and thorough execution along with a good bit of nurturing as you go. By following the advice above, you'll be clearing a path and well on the way to more engaging and productive meetings, resulting in transparency across the organization.

EXCEPTIONS ARE THE RULE

"As you can see, our company is a whole 'nother animal."

It's now been over two decades since one of us (Tor Inge) started working with software systems for business management. In his earlier days, Tor Inge worked as a practitioner, and the last twenty years as a CEO for a software company developing business management solutions. Over the years Tor Inge has received hundreds of requests for proposals (RFPs) from various customers. Many of these requests were well put together with thought-out questions related to the business need at hand; however, only a few of them focused on what can be observed in most businesses today — deviations, exceptions, and abnormalities.

As you run your business, you may feel it's very structured — organizational processes are in place and all data, goals, reporting hierarchy, and so on, can be rolled up and down perfectly. However, if you take a closer look, you will likely find instances where there are exceptions.

Let's look at some examples of typical exceptions:

- All indicators should be used by all departments — except one department.
- All limits indicating red, yellow, and green should follow this rule — except for this entity.
- All numbers should be aggregated up to total group — except for this unit.
- All KPIs should have initiatives attached to them — except for these KPIs.
- All reports should have this specific info attached — except this kind of report.
- All initiatives should have a monthly follow-up frequency — except for these months.

When it comes to how businesses are structured and operated, exceptions are the rule. Every business is unique and full of exceptions that should be considered during an RFP process. Skipping this step is what's causing problems for many businesses today. "Our system is not made for that exception, but we can maybe fix it" is the typical response you'd receive from a software vendor as the workaround development cost starts piling up.

So, the next time you find yourself drafting an RFP for a business management software, ask how exceptions are dealt with. If a vendor doesn't have a good answer, go with someone else.

Quick Tips:

If you want to find the right software vendor, you must explain your challenge clearly and ask the right questions. Here are key questions to address in your next RFP.

Tell the vendor:

- What business challenge(s) you are trying to solve
- What software (if any) you are currently using
- What the technical and/or organizational exceptions are that need to be considered
- What the must-have features and functionalities are

The better the respondents understand your request, the more accurate proposals you'll receive.

Ask the vendor:

- How does your solution solve our business challenge(s)?
- How long does it take to implement your solution?
- Does your solution integrate with existing systems?
- How do you accommodate customer requests for additional functionality?
- How do you manage software maintenance and upgrades?

- Does your company supply dedicated tech support?
- What are the tiers of support and response times? And what are the hours of operation?

The more specific questions you ask in your RFP, the better you'll be able to select a vendor that fits your specific requirements.

Next, schedule workshops with your shortlisted vendors. If possible, do this in person. Challenge the vendors with questions about exceptions specific to your business and ask them to demonstrate their answers live in the system. Seeing a live demo of the vendors' technology and testing it for yourself are the most important steps in the vendor selection process.

MANAGING CHANGE

EMBRACING VOLATILITY

"Hold my calls, Margaret! I've got some forecasting to do."

The best way to predict the future is to create it.
— Abraham Lincoln

That we live in a world of constant and upending change has been accepted as a given in every corner of our modern society. While change is often disruptive and challenging for those of us caught in its midst, what has become more troublesome in recent days is the extreme volatility associated with the changes we're witnessing — whether in climate, finance, or the business world.

Climate volatility, a touchstone in the ongoing debate over global warming, is well documented. Over the past several years, we've seen extreme weather conditions wreak havoc across the globe. Hurricanes, wildfires, extended drought conditions, and record high temperatures, just to name a few.

Given the rapid and extreme pace of change, you might logically conclude that it's more important than ever to effectively plan for the future — assessing your environment, projecting present trends, and creating a strategy that sees you vanquishing your competition and controlling your markets. Of course, we are ardent believers in strategic planning, but the realities of our ever-changing environment have forced us to re-evaluate the role of medium to long-term strategic planning in organizational success. What first caused us to shift our thinking was the realization that we, as human beings, are pitiful predictors of the future. This sad reality can be viewed both empirically — one of many studies of expert predictions discovered that over 80 percent were wrong — or by simply examining popular cultural trends: JK Rowling's original manuscript for *Harry Potter* was reportedly rejected by upward of a dozen publishing houses. This dramatic inability to predict the future presents a dilemma for strategic planners since, at its core, strategy is concerned with making predictions about the future, events that are unknowable.

So, rather than trying to predict the future with certainty, try these ideas to embrace, and even profit from, the volatility swirling about you.

1. *Examine your business – where is the most volatility occurring?*

   Cast a critical eye on the core components of your business, those that are potentially subject to the most volatility. The purpose of this exercise is to gain insights into what is happening "on the ground" around you. Here is a shortlist of the many possible volatile phenomena that may be spinning in your organizational orbit: customer preferences, employee competencies (in relation to strategy), cultural changes, global and local economy, technology, competitor actions (particularly those of new competitors), globalization, regulations, demographics, supplier relationships.

2. *Make educated guesses*

   In the previous step, we suggested you engage in detailed observations about what is occurring right now. With that perspective, shift the focus out just a bit (maybe months instead of years) and hypothesize on what is likely to take place in the immediate future. What are your customers buying? What are your competitors doing today that is impacting you? Are you surprised in any way at what is playing out around you? Why or why not? Answering these questions allows you to confront the realities of your current situation and provides you with the ammunition necessary to make more strategic decisions moving forward.

3. *Consider an "emergent strategy" approach*

   Perhaps a more suitable planning approach today is what the management scholar Henry Mintzberg described as "emergent strategy." The essence of this school of thought suggests that planners focus less on making predictions about far off events over which they have little control, and concentrate instead on reacting quickly to changes on the ground around them, thereby improving their ability to learn about what is working at this moment. One corporate example of this movement is Zara, the Spanish clothing retailer. Zara eschews the traditional process of attempting to predict next year's fashion trends, acknowledging that it basically has no idea what may be gracing the world's runways, and later its streets, in the coming months. Instead, it employs an "observe, measure, and react" strategy. As a first step, Zara sends teams of people to shopping malls, cafés, and other gathering places to see what people are currently wearing so they can quickly develop numerous ideas about what might work. Based on those "on the ground" observations, the company produces a large portfolio of styles, fabrics, and colors, all in small batches, which are quickly dispatched to stores where sales can be accurately measured. Based on the information that comes back — the react component — Zara utilizes its flexible manufacturing and distribution capabilities to respond quickly, dropping items that aren't selling and scaling up the production of those that are.

While we don't have a crystal ball at our disposal, we can increase our chances of future success by taking into account what is happening around us today, and using that knowledge to help us make informed decisions about what may in fact take place tomorrow or years down the road.

YOU'RE NOT AS CLOSE AS YOU THINK

"So that's our new strategy. Does everyone understand?"

In a separate chapter, we noted the problems that can occur when organizations developing a strategy execution system don't agree on the terminology they will employ during the process. Confusing the definitions of standard terms can lead to conflicting messages, puzzled employees, and a good deal of skepticism regarding the entire implementation.

While the effects of this nasty tendency have been apparent to us for years, it was only recently that we learned one reason why it may be so common within organizations. At the root of the problem is a phenomenon psychologists term "closeness-communication bias."[i] Simply put, the theory suggests that people commonly believe they communicate more effectively with close friends than with strangers. The belief is based on the assumption that a well-known acquaintance is in possession of the same information the speaker has, eliminating any need to provide a longer, more detailed explanation. Their shared history creates a sort of assumed shorthand, removing the necessity to fill in any blanks that may actually stand in the way of true understanding. As one researcher put it, "Our problem in communicating with friends and spouses is that we have an illusion of insight. Getting close to someone appears to create the illusion of understanding more than actual understanding."

The bias can lead to wildly inflated estimates of the ability to successfully communicate. In one simple example, researchers worked with spouses who believed they shared a solid communication footing and were always "on the same page." To test this belief, the researchers asked one spouse to utter a common term such as "It's getting hot in here" to determine if their partner was more adept at interpreting their meaning than a stranger. While the spouse uttering the phrase may have simply been suggesting the air conditioning should be switched on, the other frequently translated it as an amorous advance. As it turns out, accuracy rates for spouses and strangers were statistically identical in the study.

The research we found on this topic was restricted to close friends and spouses, but it seems logical to imagine the same pernicious effects could plague communication within organizations. Coworkers are in close proximity to one another for long periods, have a shared corporate history, and undoubtedly make assumptions about the amount and type of information possessed by their bosses, peers, and subordinates. In this context we can easily imagine a manager charged with communicating a new strategic direction to their team omitting subtle, yet important points based on their faulty assumption that the team is in possession of the same base level of information. When team members begin to make decisions that aren't consistent or, in the worst-case scenario, downright contrary to their boss's intentions, confusion and frustration are quick to appear.

To learn more about this phenomenon try:

1. *Asking your team if they feel you're all on the same page*

   Hopefully, you've created an environment in which people feel safe in suggesting they may not always fully understand the missives coming from the CEO's office.

2. *Testing it*

   If you're the team leader, write (on a flip chart or computer) your top three priorities for the next six months. Give everyone five minutes to reflect on it, then go around the room, having each person report on how they interpret the priorities. Is everyone saying the same thing? If not, you have a problem.

3. *Challenging your assumptions*

   Ask yourself what you're assuming when you share information. How much does your team really know? Could they possibly have knowledge of the subject that you're currently lacking?

The small investment you make in thinking carefully about how close you really are (from a knowledge standpoint) with your team will pay significant dividends in enhanced understanding and ultimately better results for all.

Source:

[i] See Savitsky, K., Keysar, B., Epley, N., Carter, T., & Swanson, A. (2011). The closeness-communication bias: Increased egocentrism among friends versus strangers. *Journal of Experimental Social Psychology*, 47(1), 269–273.

THIS TIME WE MEAN IT!

"A new computer?! But this one still works!"

The secret of change is to focus all of your energy, not on fighting the old, but on building the new.

— Dan Millman

Change is difficult. We all know that, right? For many of us, reluctance to change is as ingrained as breathing. Even things that could improve our lives, and that of all humanity, are initially looked at dubiously. When the telephone was introduced, it was considered "almost supernatural." At that time, hearing voices when nobody was physically present was the hallmark of insanity. And few people understood how electricity could convey a human voice. The *Providence Press* said, "It is difficult to really resist the notion that the powers of darkness are not in league with it."

One of the many problems with attempting to introduce a change in organizations is that leaders and managers fail to learn from past mistakes, using a dated playbook that dooms them to failure from the beginning. Shelves of books have been devoted to overcoming the challenges of change, so we're not suggesting we can solve the problem with five hundred words and a cartoon, but we have seen enough successful efforts to know what does work. Here are three things you can do to tilt the axis of momentum to your side the next time you roll out a new initiative.

1. *Communicate the why*

Consulting firm McKinsey has reported that

> *Most companies underestimate the importance of communicating the 'why' of a transformation; too often they assume that a letter from the CEO and a corporate slide pack will secure organizational engagement. But it's not enough to say, 'we aren't making our budget plan,' or 'we must be more competitive.' Engagement with employees and managers needs to have a context, a vision, and a call to action that will resonate with each person individually. This kind of personalization is what motivates a workforce.*

Long quote; enough said, tell people why you're changing.[i]

2. *Focus on the first ninety days*

Research indicates that more than 75 percent of people maintain a goal for a week but then they gradually slip back into old behavior. However, almost all of the people who maintain a new behavior for three months make the change permanent; the probability of relapse after that period is modest.[ii] The same applies to organizations — to make change stick you have to ingrain it into the culture, and that cultural nurturing is most critical during the first three months. It may require additional resourcing to ensure the initiative is always top of mind, but that is ultimately a small price to pay for embedding a new way of operating into the fabric of your organization.

3. *Celebrate small wins*

And the smaller the victory, the better, because it represents a chance to motivate yourself and others.[iii] It can be anything: achieving a task, holding an important meeting, solving a challenging problem. By focusing not just on the big milestone achievements, but also the day-to-day wins, you'll have more victories to celebrate, which equates to more opportunities to reinforce the change and sustain momentum. One other piece of related advice: Have fun with your celebrations. Publicly recognize people, and use a scorecard that shows just how many things you've accomplished.

As difficult as change can be to embrace, it's essential to staying ahead of the competition in today's marketplace where standing still means being passed by upstarts and rivals you didn't even see coming in your rearview mirror. Don't get left behind!

Sources:

[i] *McKinsey Quarterly*, November 2016.

[ii] *Changeology: 5 Steps to Realizing Your Goals and Resolutions.* John C. Norcross, Kristin Loberg, and Jonathon Norcross.

[iii] *Finish What You Start: The Art of Following Through, Taking Action, Executing, & Self-Discipline.* Peter Hollins.

MAKING CHANGE STICK

"Maybe we need to change our encouragement posters."

The world hates change,
yet it is the only thing that has brought progress.
— Charles Kettering

In our work we're often present at the outset of client change initiatives, whether a new measurement system or software implementation. It's exciting to be there at the beginning, when both enthusiasm and optimism are running high, and the future looks limitless. But, and here comes that understatement of all time, change is difficult — especially large-scale strategic change. Regardless of the motivation behind the change — perhaps a true burning platform that requires an imminent shift, or an exciting pivot to capture new market space — sustaining the behaviors necessary for true change is a remarkably difficult feat. Sadly, we've both witnessed this phenomenon with client firms.

Much has been written about the power of goal setting and altering habits in order to improve our personal and professional lives. However, there is compelling evidence to suggest that maintaining new behaviors is exceedingly difficult. In fact, even when their very life is on the line, people will often revert back to clearly damaging actions. Perhaps a new approach is in order.

If you're launching a new strategy, or Balanced Scorecard, OKR, or any other initiative and hoping it will dramatically alter your results, rather than relying on the vicissitudes of human nature, consider stacking the deck in your favor by altering the environment. In other words, make it easy for people to change. Here's a simple yet powerful real-world example. Virtually all school districts and public health officials would like kids to eat more vegetables in school cafeterias. To do so, some schools began experimenting with putting the trays containing veggies at the beginning of the line. Having them as a first option (rather than fries or processed meats) substantially increased the probability of kids filling at least a portion of their plates with vegetables. A simple change in the environment prompted the desired response.

What can you do to enhance the likelihood your teams will engage in desired change? Let's say you're launching a new corporate performance management system featuring a Balanced Scorecard or OKR. Your goal is to have people thinking about the vital measures that are most important to executing your strategy. Here are some easy steps that will increase the chance that those measures remain on their radar, and receive the cognitive space they need for people to act on them day in and day out.

1. *Change your meeting agendas*

   Make item one a review of your Blanced Scorecard or OKR on every management meeting agenda for the entire year. No exceptions. This sounds obvious, but we're constantly surprised by how many organizations engage in the heavy lifting of setting up a new measurement system and never go to the trouble of reviewing results.

2. *Log in to the change*

   When team members turn on their computers in the morning, the first thing they should see is your strategy, strategic measures, and so on. This may appear somewhat Orwellian at first glance, requiring your employees to sit through a corporate message before moving on to their work, but it's simply a visual cue, a reminder of what's most important. The goal is to prime people to think about what matters most as they go about their day.

3. *Decorate strategically*

   Post your strategy, your key measures of success, whatever is driving your change, prominently throughout your office in places they can't be missed. The key here is to keep it simple, displaying just the vital ingredients of your success.

The more we can remove obstacles that block desired behaviors, the better off we'll be. Altering your environment and subtly nudging people to adopt the change is an easy and cost-effective way to up the odds of a successful transformation effort.

TOO BUSY TO IMPROVE

"Can't you see we're too busy?"

You've heard this message several times throughout this section, but it's true: Change is the only constant in business. It's the fuel for growth and innovation. It's the key to gaining a competitive edge. Most organizations know that change is critical to their business's success, and yet, they struggle to embrace the concept — typically due to employee resistance.

There is no surprise here. Change is scary! There are numerous reasons why employees feel resistant toward change: fear of losing their job, fear of the unknown, fear of failure, lack of competence, lack of information, low trust in the proposed changes, and so on. It's understandable. One reason, however, that we observe way too often is stubbornness masked by excuses:

- "We don't have time to change."
- "We're too busy to learn something new."
- "We like the old way of doing things better."
- "If it ain't broke, don't fix it."

It baffles us how many organizations we've seen stuck in their status quo because they're too busy, or so they claim to be. And it's not just the employees who claim to be too busy. It's the leadership too! The reality, however, is that if you're too busy to improve, then you're too busy to succeed.

If stubbornness is what's holding you back from making changes in your organization, then you must nip it in the bud this instant! Next, consider these two tips to get you on track to successful change implementation.

1. *Develop a change plan*

   Provide an overview of the proposed change(s) and address the following questions:

   - What change(s) are you proposing?
   - Why are you proposing the change?
   - What are the benefits of the change?
   - Who is the change going to impact?
   - Who is going to carry out the change?
   - What are some of the potential risks?
   - How is the change going to be implemented?
   - How long is the implementation going to take?

2. *Communicate*

   Present the change plan to your employees. Provide your employees with context and background about the nature of the proposed change and highlight how the change is going to benefit them directly. Employees will not resist change if they believe it's in their best interest. (If the change you're proposing is not in the employees' best interest, then you have a whole other set of issues on your plate.) Use a combination of formal and informal communication and be prepared to address employees' questions and concerns.

To lead and implement change effectively takes time and communication skills. We all know that change can be a tiresome endeavor; however, in order for your business to thrive, your organization must continuously evolve. Failing to do so puts your organization at risk for losing its competitive edge and customers. Let's put it this way — *change* to keep in the step with the times, or *remain the same* and soon be left in the dust by your competition.

LET GO OF THE PAST TO THRIVE IN THE FUTURE

"I know how to turn things around! We need a social media campaign!"

Being busy does not always mean real work. The object of all work is production or accomplishment and to either of these ends there must be forethought, system, planning, intelligence, and honest purpose, as well as perspiration.

— Thomas A. Edison

As they were about to embark on a reunion tour, a reporter asked members of the legendary band The Eagles if they'd be playing just their many hits, or would also introduce new material into their sets. Don Henley answered the question by saying they would, of course, be singing their signature songs, classics like "Hotel California" and "Take it Easy," but it was also very important (and creatively rewarding) to mix in new material along the way. He said that if they sang nothing but the old songs it would quickly become boring for both them and the audience.

There's a lesson in his response for all of us: In our organizations the equivalent of "classic songs" and "hits" are the products and services we've been providing for many years and the accompanying processes we've relied on to "get things done." Sometimes we become so enamored with our classic products that they become almost sacred, and we continue to churn them out regardless of whether or not our audience — paying customers — is ready for something new and different. Take newspapers — they've been printed on large sheets of paper for centuries, but is that what customers want, or simply tradition? In this case, it's the latter. The practice of large newspapers began in London, in 1712, because the English government began taxing newspapers by the number of pages they printed. Publishers responded by printing their stories on broadsheets to minimize the number of sheets required. In 1855 the law was abolished, but the practice remained. A hundred years later, when one British company reduced the page size by half, circulation soared. Turns out people did want something new!

Peter Drucker, the original rock star management guru, coined the term "abandonment" to describe a method of periodically questioning what we sell, how we go to market, what processes we utilize, and determining whether change was necessary. He suggested you ask yourself this fundamental question: "If we weren't already in this business, would we enter it today?" He also noted that in order to grow, and growth is an imperative for virtually every organization, "A business must have a systematic policy to get rid of the outgrown, the obsolete, the unproductive."[i] Google, no slouch when it comes to winning the great game of business, is a firm believer in this concept. They conduct an annual "spring cleaning," shutting down products that are draining resources without gaining significant traction. As their former head of people operations Laszlo Bock notes, "Innovation thrives on creativity and experimentation, but it also requires thoughtful pruning."[ii]

Pruning can be a challenge, however, because the status quo exerts enormous pressure on all of us to continue down the same well-trodden path we've been walking without questioning whether it's leading us where we want and need to go. But to generate long-term success, we need to exit that gravitational pull and take a long hard look at the way we do things, and the products and services that result from our key processes.

Here are some tips to help, as you dig out your metaphorical clippers and begin pruning your menu of products, services, and processes.

1. *Remember that performance objectives and measures should be considered as well*

   An old adage reminds us "What gets measured gets managed." In other words, we tend to pay the most attention to what we're currently tracking, regardless of whether or not those indicators represent a strategy of change and innovation necessary to stay relevant in our marketplace. Critically examine your measures and ask if they provide an accurate representation of your current strategic direction. If your measures are stale, your strategy may be similarly past its expiration date.

2. *Question your assumptions*

   What are you taking for granted about the current state of your processes, products, and services? Can you validate those assumptions with data? Have you spoken with actual customers about how they use your offerings? Get out of the boardroom and into the field to ensure your assumptions are in sync with reality.

3. *Formalize and celebrate the process*

   Like Google, make this an annual event, not a one-time endeavor. Ritualize the process so that people become comfortable with the idea, and even embrace it in the spirit of progress and innovation. And keep it fun: Start a bonfire of old processes, smash decrepit products with a sledgehammer, or recite a eulogy for an outmoded service.

Remember The Eagles, and never rely exclusively on your own back catalog of "hits." Make it a discipline to periodically question the fundamental underpinnings of your business. Do so and in "The Long Run" you'll avoid a "Heartache Tonight" and can "Take It (your business) to the Limit."

Sources:

[i] http://www.inc.com/articles/2009/11/drucker.html

[ii] Bock, Laszlo (2015-04-07). Work Rules!

THE LAW OF UNINTENDED CONSEQUENCES

"Are you sure about this? I know you want to make all employees happy, but we'll probably have to replace carpets on all floors."

During the height of the global financial crisis in 2008, the CEOs of America's "Big Three" automakers: General Motors, Ford, and Chrysler, appeared before the United States Congress requesting a bailout of fifty billion dollars to keep the teetering industry afloat.[i] That's a mighty big tin cup to be rattling, and you'd expect it to be extended with a significant dose of humility. However humble the executives may have appeared in their plea to the government, their cause was significantly undermined by the fact that all three had flown to Washington on corporate jets. The lawmakers were apoplectic about this gross irony and scolded the CEOs relentlessly for their excessive spending in a time when extreme austerity was warranted.

Based on the reaction of Congress, and the public opinion nightmare that ensured, Ford CEO Alan Mulally immediately promised he would sell Ford's fleet of jets. This reaction seems logical given the maelstrom of controversy the jets had caused, but did it actually save Ford any money? No, and this is where the law of unintended consequences comes into play.

Given the fragile state of the economy at the time there were precious few buyers for a fleet of "previously enjoyed" corporate jets, and thus they sat unused in a company hangar. Of course, planes require maintenance, and Ford spent a considerable sum keeping the planes readied for potential sale. Mulally still needed to travel frequently during this period, however, and for security reasons commercial carriers were out of the question. Thus, the company spent even more money on chartered jets, and because Edsel Ford controlled the local charter company (can you say conflict of interest) the company was forced to use a service out of the area, which sent costs spiraling even higher. In the end, Ford's jet costs increased significantly, and dozens of the company's transportation employees lost their jobs.[ii] The debacle represents a quintessential example of unintended consequences in action.

This should serve as a cautionary tale to all of us. Our actions, including the measures we put in place to monitor the execution of strategy, will drive behaviors, actions, and outcomes, some that we can anticipate, but others more deleterious, that we may not foresee. Here are some suggestions for mitigating the law of unintended consequences.

1. *Make educated bets*

   Whenever we put a new system into place or begin tracking a novel metric, we're basically making a bet. We're betting that the action we're taking or the measure we're examining will lead to improved outcomes in the future. But in the end, they are just bets, or hypotheses. The best we can do is bring this notion into our consciousness at the outset of the process and attempt to anticipate all of the possible outcomes, good and bad. While we can never entirely eliminate the law of unintended consequences, we can mitigate it by including as much information as possible at the beginning of the process.

2. *Involve those impacted by the action or measure*

   It's not uncommon in any realm, politics and business being just two high profile examples, for those making decisions to be separate and distinct from those who will be affected by the decisions. Before launching an action or creating a measure, draw on the opinions and advice of those it will immediately impact. They are likely to contribute esoteric knowledge and real-world stakes that may be missing from higher-level discussions.

3. *Research what others have done*

   Chances are you're not the first to consider whatever it is you're planning to do or monitor. Look both within and outside your organization for evidence from others. What has occurred elsewhere, and how can you modify your actions to enhance the outcomes they achieved, while minimizing any negative consequences?

Unfortunately, crystal balls exist only in the world of fiction. Those glowing orbs that allow their holders the privilege of seeing the future with clarity and accuracy aren't available to those of us dwelling here on planet earth. Fortunately, such a magical device isn't necessary to avoid the pitfalls of unintended consequences. In the end, all you require is a commitment to think carefully about the ramifications of your actions.

Sources:

[i] Ford didn't require the funds, since it had already made significant cost cuts. However, it asked to be included so it wouldn't suffer unfair competition with subsidized companies.

[ii] Hoffman, Bryce G. *American Icon: Alan Mulally and the Fight to Save Ford Motor Company* (Kindle Locations 5750–5755). The Crown Publishing Group. Kindle Edition.

GOLDFISH AND STRATEGY

"I'm sorry, George. You lost me after 'welcome everyone.'"

Have you heard the statistic suggesting the average human's attention span had fallen from twelve seconds in 2000, down to just eight seconds today? The punch line was that we now have shorter attention spans than goldfish. The scientific integrity of the underlying data has since come under scrutiny, but there seems to be little doubt that, in our social media-driven, always-on world, it's become increasingly challenging to focus on any given task for a significant period of time.

Execution, however, relies heavily on strategic focus — ensuring everyone in the organization, from top to bottom is aware of your strategy, fully understands it, and determines how they can contribute to its successful delivery. In order for this to occur, you need to guarantee all teams are concentrating fully on strategic priorities, day in and day out. But here's the problem. We've both worked with companies that, in addition to sharing strategy with their workforces, also bombard them with core competencies, values, strategic imperatives, standards, and many other seemingly important accouterments of corporate achievement. If I'm an employee, to which of these do I align my actions? They all "seem" important, they're in binders on a shelf after all. So, what do I do? This confusion leads, not surprisingly, to redundancies of effort, confusion, and poor results.

If you want to break from the pack, job number one is clearing the path for your employees by creating a differentiating strategy and ensuring everyone grasps both its overall meaning and its implications for them. Here are some ideas to help you along the way.

1. *Conduct an audit*

   Besides strategy, what other "critical" messages have you shared with your team. Catalog them and critically review each. Do they align with one another? Are all of them truly necessary or do they simply produce confusion? If they aren't helping you on the execution front, do yourself a favor and toss them on the junk heap of well-intentioned but ultimately unhelpful ideas.

2. *Have fun with it*

   Some organizations will take the opportunity to transform this corporate pruning exercise into an entertaining ceremony. We know of one company that created a roaring bonfire fed exclusively with any unnecessary and contradictory directives from leadership.

3. *Use the oldest trick in the book*

   And that is repetition. Once you've pruned the terminology tree, focus on one thing — your core strategy — and share it with people over and over and over again. We've heard CEOs of successful companies say they were almost physically ill because they repeated the elements of the strategy so often. However, that's the commitment required to ensure your precise message is getting through to an often tragically distracted workforce.

It's getting harder all the time to grab someone's attention and hold it for any reasonable amount of time. The competition for cognitive real estate is immense and powerfully armed with dopamine-driving clickbait, startling statistics, and endless kitten memes vying for our mental bandwidth. Sorry for the cliché, but now more than ever you must be sure your communication is targeted to the information your teams really need.

COMPARING APPLES AND EXECUTION

"Tonight I'll start my new running regimen."

Execution is a specific set of behaviors and techniques that companies need to master in order to have competitive advantage. It's a discipline of its own.

— Ram Charan and Larry Bossidy, Execution

This chapter is directly from Paul.

As a busy consultant with clients around the globe, I spend a lot of nights in hotel rooms, and over the years have developed my share of routines. I've established habits for things like: What order to unpack in, where I put my things, what side of the bed I sleep on, and so on. My routine even extends to the ritual for checking out, which always starts with running over a checklist before I leave my room. Do I have my keys (if renting a car)? Have I left anything in the room? Is my phone charger (it's the No. 1 item left in hotel rooms) unplugged and in my backpack? Satisfied I'm ready to leave, I head out the door, and away I go.

On a recent trip, as I was dutifully going through my pre-exit checklist, a thought bubbled up from my growling tummy, *I'm hungry*. No problem I figured, I'll stop by the buffet on my way to the reception desk and grab an apple. Satisfied I'd solved that problem, I finalized the checklist, turned out the light and headed for the elevator. Just a few minutes later I was sitting in my rented Nissan Sentra en route to the client's office. But, do you think I had an apple with me? The answer, sadly for my empty stomach, is no. Now you could say that I'm just absentminded or was in a rush to make sure I was on time for the meeting, but there is a scientific reason for my forgetfulness. Because I was hungry I *intended* to pick up an apple on the way to reception. However, I normally don't get apples on my way to check out, and thus the force of my very ingrained checkout habit was exponentially stronger than my immediate intention. Turns out that regardless of the situation, whenever our habits are stronger than our intentions, habits will invariably win.

So, what does this have to do with strategy execution? When we embark on an execution program, with the Balanced Scorecard or OKR, we're launching a change initiative whether we label it that or not. We're changing the way we measure performance, the way we conduct conversations, and if done well, we're changing our ability to align, engage, and execute for the better. In order to make that change happen, we have to begin to ingrain new habits into our culture: how we do things day in and day out. In other words, OKRs have to vie against the current habits we've built up over the entire time we've been in operation, and those typically run deep. Very deep. How do we begin to sew OKR or the Balanced Scorecard into the fabric of our organizations? Well, let's return to me and my apple. If there had been apples on the reception desk, or if I'd had to walk past the buffet to get to the desk, the likelihood of me remembering to pick one up would have risen considerably. So, speaking metaphorically, we need to put the OKR or Balanced Scorecard apple in front of people to start building that habit.

Here are a few things you can do to start making strategy execution a healthy habit at your organization:

1. *Build on habits you already have*

   Scientists call this "habit stacking," adding a desired new habit to one you currently practice. For example, I'm pretty certain you have management meetings of some kind now. Take a portion of that time to discuss your new goals, or better yet, use those new goals to drive the meeting agenda.

2. *Make it easy for people to access their own, and others', goals*

   Don't bury goals five levels down in some dusty, rarely used corporate intranet you last updated with meaningful information in 1998. Bring them front and center for all to see and discuss. There are many robust software platforms that make transparency and accessibility a breeze. Ensure your teams post their goals to a common repository so that review and analysis are simple for everyone. And don't forget the old-school possibilities of poster-sized versions of your goals on office walls.

3. *Start small*

   One key to successfully launching any new habit is establishing quick wins through realistic action. If you're out of shape, you wouldn't charge into the gym, throw 225 pounds on the bar and expect to press it a dozen times. Try that and you'd surrender after one doomed repetition. Instead, start with a reasonable goal you're likely to achieve. In goals parlance this translates to a couple of things: Keep the number of goals small at the outset. Don't burden yourself with too many. And, as noted above, make them aspirational but ultimately achievable.

They say you can't compare apples and oranges, but I hope in this short article you've learned that you can compare apples and execution. If you want to succeed, keep the goals apple in front of everyone at all times, and before you know it, the habit will be in place.

MANAGEMENT & LEADERSHIP

EVERYONE WATCHES WHAT THE BOSS WATCHES

"But you also better meet your sales goals!" '

The challenge of leadership is to be strong, but not rude;
be kind, but not weak; be bold, but not bully;
be thoughtful, but not lazy; be humble, but not timid;
be proud, but not arrogant; have humor, but without folly.

— Jim Rohn

We've both had the chance to attend many conferences and seminars over the years and have enjoyed hearing organizations regale the audience with their successful applications of Balanced Scorecard, OKR, and numerous other execution systems. While every story is unique and stresses different aspects of the implementation, what they share in common is this: Every successful endeavor enjoyed one crucial element — the sponsorship of their senior executive in both words and actions.

The American television evangelist Joel Osteen once noted, when referring to how our actions affect our children, that "Kids are like little video cameras with legs." They're constantly recording what's taking place around them, monitoring what their parents are doing, and to the best of their abilities, modeling that behavior. Of course, we're not comparing employees to children, but the analogy holds. As members of a team, we look for signals from those whose opinion matters most when it comes to steering the ship, and in virtually all organizations that person is the chief executive officer. We're recording their actions; how consistent they are, what they're saying about what's important, where our focus should be. As the title of this piece implies, everyone watches what the boss watches. Or another favorite cliché, "If it interests my boss, it fascinates me."

With strategy execution, perhaps the single most important element of success is aligning everyone in the organization around a stated course of action. If, however, the CEO says one thing and then does another — perhaps (as the cartoon implies) enthusiastically touting the benefits of being customer focused, but then chastising any group that doesn't hit their numbers regardless of customer satisfaction — this creates discord, confusion, and skepticism.

If you're a CEO, or any leader for that matter, consider the following to ensure you're saying and doing the right things.

1. *Commit to your strategy*

   Before you begin communicating with your teams, you must do the heavy lifting of creating a strategy you believe carves the best path forward for your organization. And this means being personally involved and not ceding responsibility to, for example, an outside consultant. External expertise can help by outlining challenges and identifying opportunities, but in the end, the CEO and senior leadership must weigh the evidence and personally commit to a strategic direction. The act of personal involvement will help ensure both a depth of understanding and commitment to the strategy.

2. *Communicate ceaselessly*

   Once you've put a strategic stake in the ground, communicate it frequently, whenever possible personally delivering the message to employees. The more you share, the more you internalize the message. Also, by inviting questions you galvanize your resolve and develop even deeper insights into why the chosen path was selected.

3. *Ask for feedback*

    The simplest and best way to ensure you're being consistent in words and actions (beyond your own observations) is to ask those you work with and rely on to share your messages to a wider audience. Is what you're doing on a day-to-day basis consistent with what you've publicly shared as the organization's direction? If not, what impact is that having on your direct reports, and other managers as they attempt to translate what they're seeing to frontline staff hungry for a consistent message. To be frank, this will require a level of trust and transparency that does not exist in all organizations. However, given the blinders most of us wear when it comes to our actual versus desired behavior, it is vital should you hope to garner useful insights.

It's a fact of organizational life that in both good times and bad, we look to our leaders for cues. If you're saying one thing, but doing another that inconsistency will soon manifest in confusion, skepticism, and ultimately subpar performance.

CONTROL FREAKS

"It's called managing by lurking around."

Management is, above all, a practice where art, science, and craft meet.
— Henry Mintzberg

Over the course of our professional lives, we have come across a lot of managers. Some good, and some not so much. There were the charismatic types, the visionaries, the compromisers, the nurturers, the showboats, the absentees, the know-it-alls, the drill sergeants, the micromanagers, the fast talkers, and those who never said much at all. As a CEO of an organization, Tor Inge also had the opportunity to interview and employ a fair share of managers and later watch them in action.

While most of the managers Tor Inge hired were able to successfully lead their teams, others were not so successful. What he observed is that, what he calls, "control freak" managers had a lot less success in keeping their teams happy and motivated. There are two types of "control freak" managers:

1. *The "lack of trust" control freaks*

   These managers tend to lack general trust in their employees. They over-supervise their teams to ensure that work gets done, but rarely give praise or recognition. Often these managers are very skilled in their field of expertise, but their management approach hinders team morale and negatively impacts productivity.

2. *The "insecure" control freaks*

   These managers are a true challenge to work for. These managers have low competence and skill set to get a job done, so they hide it by oppressing their teams with rigid systems of control and silence. They are political in nature and very cautious about what information they release and what they keep to themselves.

The managers you bring on board play an important role in carrying out your organizational strategy and have a big impact on how employees feel about coming to work, their job, and the company as a whole. There are a lot of people who call themselves *good* managers but have zero interest in the good of the company. Being able to identify the truly good ones is vital to your organization's success. Look for those individuals who display genuine care for employee wellness and your organization's best interests. There is a popular saying that goes "employees don't quit their jobs, they quit their managers." So, the next time you're looking for a new manager, be sure to keep an eye out for the "control freaks." They can ruin your company!

AVOIDING GROUPTHINK

"Everyone in favor raise your hand!"

All of us are not always smarter than one of us, leaders need to distinguish between the wisdom of crowds and the madness of crowds.

— Paul Gibbons

Quick quiz: What do Watergate, the Bay of Pigs disaster, and the escalation of the Vietnam War have in common? Answer: They're all consequences of the phenomenon known as "groupthink." The examples cited above are well-known policy blunders, but groupthink is certainly not limited to the halls of government. Chances are you've experienced or witnessed it in your own organizational environment. Groupthink is characterized by a cohesive group's desire for unanimity above all else. When the phenomenon takes hold, members of the group will suppress conflicting opinions, avoid evaluation of alternative courses of action, rationalize in order to discount outside warnings, and ultimately be much more likely to make risky (and sometimes unethical) decisions.

In his seminal book on the topic, Irving L. Janis carefully enumerates the tragic outcomes of the policy decisions noted above, consistently demonstrating the role groupthink played in the deliberations of otherwise astute and intelligent men. For example, he notes that when President John F. Kennedy and his inner circle were making plans for the doomed Bay of Pigs invasion in Cuba, the group made six assumptions — each unquestioned and unchallenged — that all later proved to be incorrect. Each member of the team later documented their private misgivings, but noted that the power of cohesion within the group was so strong, dissenting viewpoints were never uttered, and thus serious debate was muted.

As noted above, the prevalence of groupthink is also alive and well in many organizational boardrooms. Despite calls for diversity, many executives tend to surround themselves with like-minded thinkers who are unlikely to deviate from the gravitational pull of the team. This often results in risky or unethical actions that fail to receive the proper scrutiny they deserve before being initiated.

Prior to launching any major initiative or strategic shift, here are some tips to ensure your team is not falling prey to the many harmful effects of groupthink.

1. *Assign a "devil's advocate"*

   Have one member of the group assume the role of contrarian, critically examining the team's decisions and offering conflicting points of view. This advocate need not be strident or rude, but simply raise new issues by asking basic questions such as "Shouldn't we give some thought to …?" "Have we considered …?" "Are we overlooking …?" In order for this role to prove effective, however, it is crucial that the team's leader genuinely support it and allow for dissenting opinions to surface. If it's a "token" role, results won't change.

2. *Hold a "second chance" meeting*

   Group cohesion is so powerful that in the moment it will often suppress even the most vocal critics of a proposed decision. Therefore, to be certain there is true unanimity around a course of action, before the final vote is taken or decision made, the leader should instruct each member of the team to reflect on the discussions in a different environment. Away from the often dissent-stifling confines of a conference room, team members can critically challenge the decisions, call on outside experts, and yes, even sleep on it, before reconvening to come to a final conclusion.

3. *If all else fails, drink some wine*

   In his book, Janis notes that whenever ancient Persians made a decision following sober deliberations, they would always reconsider it under the influence of wine. This being a cartoon book we expect you to take that advice for what it's worth and also consider the possible impact of what is colloquially known as "drinking thinking."

Humans are social creatures, and whether at work or play, we naturally align in groups. Teams, families, clubs; they're all comforting and supportive structures for our psyches, but in these environments it's easy to fall under the spell of cohesion and consensus, often resulting in suboptimal decisions resulting from groupthink. Keep your eyes open to the impact of groupthink in your team, and your decisions will be better for it.

Source:

The text above draws on Irving L. Janis, *Group-Think*. Boston, MA, Houghton Mifflin Company, 1983.

HOW TO BUILD TRUST IN YOUR ORGANIZATION

"Of course, we trust you! The company ankle monitor is just for your safety and protection."

We all know how important trust is to any relationship, whether personal or professional. Without the bond afforded by trust, the floorboards are, to say the least, very loose beneath us. Regardless of industry, today's enterprises rely heavily on employees working collaboratively across functions to drive business results, and trust is the fuel that makes these relationships work.

When trust is present, results flourish. Employees in high-trust organizations are more productive, have more energy at work, collaborate better with their colleagues, stay longer, and compared with people at low-trust organizations, report 74 percent less stress. It appears that most organizations recognize the benefits afforded by increased trust and are aware of the potential threats accompanying a lack thereof. In a global CEO survey, PricewaterhouseCoopers (PwC) reported that 55 percent of companies think a lack of trust is a threat to their organization's growth. But most have done little to increase it.

If your organization is among the majority that has yet to invest in the power of trust, try these tips to enhance its presence.

1. *Set challenging goals*

   One way to increase trust in the workplace is to introduce challenging, but achievable goals. The moderate stress of the assignment releases neurochemicals, including oxytocin, that intensify focus and power social connections, driving cross-functional collaboration in the process. However, the effect is only possible if the goals are attainable and have a concrete endpoint.

2. *Give employees a say in what they work on*

   When employees are given the opportunity to choose the projects they work on, energy, focus, and trust increase substantially. Autonomy is a powerful driver of motivation and commitment.

3. *Share information broadly*

   This next statistic is one that is sadly endemic in the corporate world: Only 40 percent of employees report they are well informed about their company's goals, strategies, and tactics. Uncertainty about the company's overall direction leads to chronic stress, undermines teamwork, and reduces trust.

This last point deserves additional attention. Much of this book is focused on the power of measuring your strategy through tools like OKR and the Balanced Scorecard. Let's take OKR for example. The power of the framework is derived in large part from teams across the organization creating OKRs that signal their unique contribution to the firm's overall strategic goals. And the fact of the matter is this: no team can create a truly effective OKR without knowledge of the company's strategy. Therefore, before launching an OKR program, be sure you've communicated your strategy widely — reaching the entire workforce. Most frontline employees will seek information from their direct supervisors, so be certain this critical audience is particularly familiar with the strategy and consistent in how they discuss it. And once you have strategy-based OKRs, share them! One of Google's OKR best practices is complete transparency. Literally everyone can see anyone else's OKRs. This boosts collaboration, productivity, and trust.

Source:

The tips above are based on material presented in "The Neuroscience of Trust" by Paul J. Zak, appearing in the January–February 2017 issue of the *Harvard Business Review*.

THE PRICE OF INCIVILITY IN THE WORKPLACE

"I know I've been rude, unfair, and overbearing. It's called coaching."

Clients do not come first. Employees come first. If you take care of your employees, they will take care of the clients.
— Richard Branson

Not long ago one of us (Paul) visited a pharmacy in his town and came across a tall, late middle-aged man with gray hair, mean eyes, and a menacing expression on his face. Think Mr. Gower at the beginning of the movie *It's a Wonderful Life*. Turns out this gentleman was the store manager. I was at the cash register, paying, when he marched over to the cashier, thrust a huge tub of hand sanitizer in her palm and commanded (in front of all the customers): "Use this … you know why!" And in case you're wondering, this was before the Covid-19 pandemic. Then he left from behind the counter and barked: "Oh, it's mister I can't work on Tuesdays" to some hapless teenage worker who was cleaning the floor. The employee muttered a somewhat pathetic, "What?" to which the manager replied, "Mister I can't work on Tuesdays. Thanks for gracing us with your presence today." The obviously disgruntled employee mumbled something to himself and skulked off with his mop. That must be a fun place to work, huh?

The sad part is that it's not that different from many workplaces in our fast-paced world that often place a premium on speed and "getting things done" over respect and courtesy. Incivility is on a rapid ascent in the modern workplace, with the share of employees who report being treated rudely by colleagues at least once a month increasing from 49 percent in 1998 to 62 percent in 2016. Chances are you've probably witnessed, experienced, or (difficult as it is to admit) committed an uncivil act in the last thirty days. Hypotheses abound to explain the uptick: the use of email replacing face-to-face communication (it's always easier to be rude when hiding behind a cyber curtain), overburdened managers taking their frustrations out on employees, simmering culture clashes due to globalization, and many others. While the causes aren't always clear, there is little doubt about the consequences.

It's not just someone's pride or ego that takes a beating when subjected to incivility. Performance suffers commensurately. Thirty-eight percent of those who were treated poorly at work said they intentionally decreased the quality of their work going forward. Additionally, a whopping 78 percent said their commitment to the organization had decreased. And, echoing my encounter at the drugstore, consumers are less likely to purchase from a company they perceive as uncivil, regardless of whether the rudeness is directed at them or employees. Here are a few tips to stop incivility from gaining a foothold in your workplace.

1. *Prevent it from starting in the first place*

   Make civility and treating others with respect and dignity a core tenet of your culture, and interview for it with prospective employees. Check references carefully, ask questions that will provide hints of the person's true proclivities, and never underestimate the power of intuition. If something doesn't feel right, it probably isn't.

2. *Wield your "power" carefully*

   If you're in a position of authority, studies have demonstrated that regardless of how kindly and empathetically you've acted in the past, enhanced power can lead you to exercise less empathy, exploit others, and focus on your own needs first. Be cognizant of this possibility and engage in the thought exercise of imagining the kind of person you want to be, how you'd like to be viewed by others, then ensure your behavior is consistent with those desires. Humility goes a long way and allowing others to respectfully challenge your thinking can be a triple win — for you, them, and the organization in the form of more innovative thinking.

3. *Provide tools to help people*

   In one survey, 25 percent of those who were asked why they were uncivil blamed the organization for not providing the skills they required. This is easily remedied with training on giving and receiving feedback respectfully, how to handle difficult conversations, and coaching on constructive ways for dealing with stress.

We spend a third (or more) of our lives at work. By following just a few simple steps we can ensure those hours lead to a sense of satisfaction and fulfillment, rather than humiliation, fear, and contempt resulting from toxic interactions with jaded bosses and colleagues.

Sources:

Christine Porath, "The hidden toll of workplace incivility." *McKinsey Quarterly*, December 2016.

Robert Sutton, "Memo to the CEO: Are you the source of workplace dysfunction?" *McKinsey Quarterly*, September 2017.

ARE YOU GETTING THE MOST FROM YOUR MANAGEMENT MEETINGS?

"Now that we're done discussing last night's game, let's vote on whether we should end this meeting."

We live in polarizing times — whether it's politics, sports, or Wall Street, opinion tends to split down the middle with half the population supporting one view and the other vehemently defending the alternative. But differences of opinion vanish when you bring up meetings. Most people agree they're of questionable value, and have plenty (to put it mildly) of room for improvement. Need some proof? In a recent survey of 182 senior managers from a range of industries:

- 71% said meetings are unproductive and inefficient
- 65% complained that meetings keep them from completing their own work
- 64% said meetings come at the expense of deep thinking

In another study, 90 percent of people reported daydreaming in meetings and 73 percent admitted they use meeting time to do other work. Finally, that same study proclaimed the existence of the very malignant sounding "meeting recovery syndrome." It suggests the effects of a bad meeting can linger for hours in the form of participant grousing and complaining.

We could fill this entire book on statistics that outline the many grievances associated with meetings. But, let's be honest, meetings aren't going anywhere. Every day here in the United States there are about eleven million of them taking place, so it's difficult to envision a future in which we don't convene to discuss matters of mutual interest.

Are meetings all bad? We don't think so, and in fact we'll go so far as to say they play a critical role in the achievement of goals. To discover why, we need to burrow down a bit of a neuroscience rabbit hole. Researchers tell us that when it comes to goals, our brains work on a very fundamental premise: discrepancies must be reduced. The goal is where we want to go, what we want to achieve. Luckily for the striving mammals we are, our brains can quickly determine the gap between that desired end state and our current position. It then wants to take necessary actions to close the gap, thus reducing discrepancies. And what is one of the critical ways it does that? By analyzing feedback on those actions. It's pretty much impossible to achieve any goal without a sense of how we're doing, how we're progressing. And, coming full circle now, meetings are an outstanding forum for providing, discussing, and analyzing feedback on goals, whether corporate, team, or individual.

Hopefully, you can now see the potential of good meetings. Try these three tips to improve your next gathering:

1. *Create and stick to a focused agenda*

   Everyone wants to be efficient with their time, but you simply can't cover everything from strategy reviews to monthly operating results to the latest IT initiatives in one sitting without sacrificing quality dialog for speed. That's the meeting equivalent of multitasking, but recent research on brain science is shedding new light on the long-accepted virtues of multitasking. Turns out we *can't* do two things at once, and attempting to do so actually harms productivity. Your first responsibility in bringing your colleagues to the table for a meeting is to have a focused agenda that concentrates on a limited number of related subjects, or maybe just one, allowing time for analysis, discussion, and learning.

2. *Listen more, talk less*

   When we sit in on client meetings it sometimes occurs to us that everyone around the table is just waiting, very impatiently, for a chance to speak. When that time comes, based on the new direction in which they spin the conversation, it's pretty obvious they didn't really hear a word the previous speaker uttered, and are simply intent on getting their point across. In your next meeting, we encourage you to take the time to really listen to your colleagues' point of view and, as Benjamin Franklin once noted: "Gain knowledge by use of the ear, rather than the tongue." Before providing your own opinion, share what you believe you heard others say and don't progress until you can express it to their satisfaction.

3. *Score the meeting's effectiveness*

   After the meeting, ask participants to rate its effectiveness on a number of predetermined criteria. The dimensions you choose to measure are up to you, but consider the following to get your creative juices flowing: Did the meeting begin and end on time? Were materials provided in advance? Did the facilitator review the agenda? Did the facilitator guide the discussion effectively? Was there active participation from all participants? Were actions recorded? Keep track of responses over time to determine whether or not your meetings are becoming more effective as judged by participants. To keep things really simple, try giving everyone a single piece of paper at the end of the meeting, have them record their thoughts, and drop the paper in one of two buckets, "Cheers" or "Jeers."

The comedian Dave Barry has this to say on the topic: "If you had to identify, in one word, the reason why the human race has not achieved, and never will achieve, its full potential, that word would be 'meetings.' " Harsh words, but funny. Of course, it doesn't have to be that way. Follow the steps above to get your meetings back on track.

Sources:

First three meeting statistics: "Want to run a good meeting? First, take a comedy class." *Wall Street Journal.* October 31, 2018.

Final two meeting statistics: Steven G. Rogelberg, "Why Your Meetings Stink — And What To Do About It." *Harvard Business Review.* January–February, 2019.

Brain science: Heidi Grant Halvorson, *Succeed.* Hudson Street Press. 2010.

LOCATION, LOCATION, LOCATION

"Isn't this a great location?"

Creativity is intelligence having fun.
— Albert Einstein

It's the first rule of real estate: location, location, location. The most desirable properties, those that command the highest prices, are inevitably situated in the best locations. But does location play a role when it comes to your next meeting to craft a new strategy, or determine the performance measures you'll use to gauge strategy execution? While there are undoubtedly people out there who think it matters very little whether you hold your meetings in your own conference rooms, the closest coffee shop, or the basement of a community center, we think it does impact both creativity and results.

Let's start with a fairly mundane, but nonetheless important and practical, reason to consider going offsite for your next important meeting. As facilitators this is an area we're very familiar with and we can both say unequivocally that probably the least favorite aspect of our job is chasing workshop participants down after breaks. We've logged the equivalent of marathons patrolling corridors and poking into offices urging reluctant attendees back to the meeting. It's not necessarily the meeting itself that causes their tardiness, but the force field of their own offices and the thousand things screaming for attention within its four walls that prevent them from coming back on time. Holding meetings offsite solves this problem in an instant. OK, check. Now let's get on to the much more captivating reason to escape your own building.

And that is creativity! For many people, corporate meeting rooms carry with them the stigma of long, dry, and useless information exchanges, and wastes of never-to-be-retrieved time. It's difficult to be innovative and creative in a space you associate with such negative experiences. So, go offsite, but where? We know what you're thinking — a hotel or resort. That should do the trick, right? Maybe, but we've got what we think is an even better idea. Pick a company in your area that you admire, or one you feel offers the possibility of lessons you can apply to your organization, and ask if you can use space at their facility. That's exactly what John Sztykiel did when he was CEO of Spartan Motors, a specialty automotive company in Charlotte, Michigan.[i] Wanting to shake things up, he approached nearby manufacturer Peckham, Inc. about holding a meeting in their location. Peckham was known as an environmentally friendly, energy-efficient manufacturer, and Mr. Sztykiel felt there was much his team could learn from them. Thinking it may help their business as well, Peckham agreed.

Spartan held their strategy meeting at Peckham, and during a break, while touring the manufacturing facility Mr. Sztykiel noticed piles of fabric within walking distance of the forklift and the manufacturing area. The fabric got cut within twenty yards of the shelves where it is stored. That got him and his team to consider ways they could reduce distances at Spartan. They decided to move materials storage closer to their manufacturing facility, and began looking for closer suppliers to reduce delivery times, both actions resulting in significant savings. By the way, the total cost for the meeting was $87 (breakfast and lunch). Talk about return on investment!

So, before you have your assistant book a hotel for your next offsite, try this instead:

1. *Share the idea*

   Outline the issues that arise when holding meetings at your location, and share the possibility of going offsite, but differently!

2. *Brainstorm a list of local businesses that are a good fit for you*

   Those within easy driving distance that you can learn from and to which you could also potentially add value, or even partner with at some point in the future.

3. *Commit to learning*!

   You're asking a favor of another business for a reason — to spark creativity and generate results. Be sure to take time when at another location to tour the facility, ask questions, and then apply what you've learned to your own business.

Location isn't something reserved for choosing your next house. Marshaling the creativity and enthusiasm of your team when tackling a challenging problem or exploring exciting opportunities can be impacted by the venue you select, so choose wisely.

Source:

[i] This story is based on an article that originally appeared in the *Wall Street Journal* on March 8, 2010.

THE DOWNSIDE OF WORKING LUNCHES

"Taking a break for lunch are you Anderson? It must be nice not to have anything better to do."

Over the past two decades, we've facilitated thousands of workshops with organizations around the world. During these sessions clients engage in the significant mental effort required to build systems that will lead to the execution of their strategies. It's hard work, intellectually demanding and often tiring, but ultimately rewarding when the entire team lands on the same strategic page, understanding exactly what success looks like and how they'll achieve it.

When the clock ticks close to noon during these events, it's very common for participants to meet calls for a lunch break with a few sneers and remarks that suggest the not so subtle subtext of "We're professionals, we don't need a lunch break … let's power through this!" The desire to capitalize on the momentum accumulated during the morning session is understandable, and we applaud the work ethic of those wanting to carry on without a break. However, as a mounting body of research indicates, working through lunch is simply not a good idea for you, or your organization.

That is, if you're even lucky enough to have a lunch break. Some recent estimates suggest that just one in five office workers is taking a break away from their desk. Again, that's a mistake. Chris Cunningham, a professor at the University of Tennessee, is one of many researchers who believe a midday break is essential in restoring the energy and focus necessary to tackle the pressing problems most of us encounter in our day-to-day work lives. "The attention it takes to focus at work drains (people) of psychological, social, and material reserves, leading to stress and lower productivity. Taking a lunch break away from the desk lets people separate themselves from the source of that drain." [i]

Concentration, cognitive capacity, and the willpower necessary to forge ahead on tasks are all limited resources that we deplete during the day. Without a break (or breaks) we exhaust those reserves, diminishing our ability to be creative and problem-solve effectively — the very currency of modern productivity and effectiveness. Do yourself a favor, when noon rolls around, instead of plowing ahead, try these ideas instead.

1. *Take a walk*

   The evidence on movement is clear and compelling. Getting out and simply walking for a short period of time can improve brain function, lower anxiety, and recharge your cognitive battery for the rest of the day. The benefits are even greater if you have access to nature. Compare that with the alternative of sitting at your desk. Research from the Mayo Clinic has linked sitting for extended periods of time with a number of significant health concerns including obesity and metabolic syndrome, a deleterious band of conditions including high blood pressure, high blood sugar, excess body fat around the waist, and abnormal cholesterol levels. As if that weren't bad enough, the research also suggests that sitting too much can increase the risk of death from cardiovascular disease and cancer.

2. *Eat*!

   Given our hyper-busy lives, many of us have neglected the "lunch" in lunch break. Rather than enjoy some nourishing food, we take the opportunity to run errands, squeeze in a workout, or of course continue working. However, to function effectively our bodies require fuel. But hold on, that doughnut or candy bar from the office vending machine, the one that spikes your glucose levels for thirty minutes before leading to an inevitable crash, it doesn't count. Try whole foods, mostly plant-based, instead.

3. *Socialize*

   Our first piece of advice was to get outside and walk, so why not magnify its positive effects by combining it with a little quality time shared with coworkers or friends whose company you enjoy.

If there is one thing pretty much everyone can agree on these days, it's the fact that — despite the many labor-saving devices omnipresent in our lives — we're all busier than ever. Powering through your day without stopping may be efficient in the short term, but for the sake of your long-term health and productivity, do yourself a favor and take a little break from time to time.

Source:

[i] Making the Most of Your Lunch Hour, *Wall Street Journal*, October 8, 2013.

LEARN MORE IN LESS TIME

"Almost caught up on my reading!"

Paul recently heard a TV executive say that between broadcast networks, cable, and streaming outlets there are over five hundred scripted shows running in the United States right now. Over five hundred! How are we supposed to keep up with them? Every time we chat with friends, a new show will surface in the conversation. "Have you seen …?" "No," we'll reply. "How about …?" Again, the inevitable answer is, "No." How could we? There are over five hundred and only so many hours in the day.

The frightening thing is that five hundred actually represents a relatively reasonable number when you compare it to the literal avalanche of interesting books (whether business, fiction, biography, etc.), articles, blog posts, and so on that is published daily and scream for our attention. As a manager or leader, it's critical that you stay current on the latest trends in not only your own industry, but business in general. This is especially the case now — an exciting time in the management field with novel insights being gleaned from emerging disciplines such as neuroscience, behavioral economics, and many others. To take advantage of the findings you must first, of course, consume the content. Although it's ultimately a wise investment, in the short term it places yet another demand on your scarcest resource — time.

So how *do* we keep up? The answer is to be more discriminating before, during, and after you read. Here are three tips to get you started:

1. *Focus on purpose*

   Before you commit to reading something, ask yourself about the purpose of doing so. "Why should I read this particular item right now?" The more specific you are when answering the question, the better. Dig deep to determine whether reading it will help you with a current issue or challenge, or generally improve your professional or personal life in some way. We know what you're thinking — reading is its own reward. And that's true — to a point. However, given the mountains of material we all need to get through in the run of a day, it pays, and is ultimately more rewarding, to only read what holds potential value for you at the moment. If it doesn't have a purpose, toss it!

2. *Track the value add*

   If you've found something that passes the purpose test, be sure to keep that value in mind as you're reading. In fact, you may want to actually write it on the first page to remind yourself why you've made this substantial investment. As you read, return to that statement of purpose frequently to put the material in context and ensure you're getting as much out of the text as possible. Taking handwritten notes while reading will also pay extensive dividends in understanding and application.

3. *Apply what you've learned quickly*

   One of the best ways to do that is through business guru Stephen Covey's process of "Third-Person Teaching." Share what you read with others, conveying the key points and what you personally gained from them. If the reading is professional in nature, consider starting a book club or "lunch and learn" to discuss important topics and how they could be applied in your organization. Or, if you feel the topic has immediate relevance, discuss it at your next team meeting and challenge the group to determine how you could apply the principles in a meaningful and effective way.

Hopefully you find these tips helpful. There is more we could say on the topic, but we have to go. Just heard about a really good new TV show!

RUNNING FASTER OR SMARTER

"And that's Steve. He never gets any work done, but he can type very fast."

Efficiency and focus are the keys to success.

— Robert Crais

Have you ever heard your boss saying that your organization needs to "Become more productive? Work harder? Be more efficient?" Hearing such pronouncements has the potential to send many people into instant panic mode. "The management thinks I'm too slow. I need to work faster! My job depends on it!" The truth, however, is that efficiency and productivity have little to do with how fast we work. Simply adding speed to our work processes does not necessarily result in us being more productive.

Efficiency and productivity come from the following:

1. Making sure what you do contributes to fulfilling your company's strategy. (Justified by strategy — adding value)
2. What you do — do it right. (Right quality)
3. How you do it — do it the right way. (Right process)
4. Prioritizing initiatives and choosing which ones to do first, second, and which ones to never do. (Project management)
5. Making sure what you do can be justified economically. (Financial management)
6. Making sure that you have the needed skills to perform the job. (HR management)
7. Making sure that what you do has acceptable risk. (Risk management)

None of the seven items on the list asks you to "run faster." The key to productivity and efficiency is doing the right things and doing them well. Stay focused, keep your distractions under control, prioritize, and remember to take breaks. Learning to be more efficient and productive will not only ease the stress of your job, but it will also make you a more valuable asset for your company.

ABOUT THE AUTHORS

PAUL NIVEN

Paul Niven is a management consultant, author, and noted speaker on the subjects of strategy, strategy execution, objectives and key results (OKR), and the Balanced Scorecard (BSC). As both a practitioner and consultant he has developed successful strategy execution systems for clients large and small in a wide variety of organizations, including Fortune 1000 companies, public sector, and nonprofit agencies. Paul is the founder of both OKRsTraining.com and The Senalosa Group. The companies have assisted over five hundred organizations around across the globe effectively execute their strategy. A small sample of clients includes: CNN, Humana, Mercedes-Benz, Anheuser-Busch, Adidas, Hulu, Facebook, and the United States Navy.

Paul has always enjoyed writing and in 2001 was approached by editors at John Wiley and Sons to write a practical "how-to" book on implementing the Balanced Scorecard. The subsequent book, *Balanced Scorecard Step-by-Step: Maximizing Performance and Maintaining Results*, has since been translated into over fifteen languages around the world and continues to be a trusted guide for organizations utilizing the scorecard approach. Paul subsequently wrote three additional books on the Balanced Scorecard and a business fable, *Roadmaps and Revelations*, designed to take the mystery out of the strategic planning process. Paul's most recent book, co-authored with Ben Lamorte is *Objectives and Key Results: Driving Focus, Alignment, and Engagement with OKRs*, a practical guide to creating OKRs.

You can reach Paul at pniven@senalosa.com.

TOR INGE VASSHUS

Tor Inge Vasshus is the founder and CEO of Corporater — a global software company that enables medium and large organizations to manage their entire business on a single platform. He is an experienced practitioner of management methodologies, a dynamic speaker on the topics of technology trends and integrated software solutions, and a trusted strategy advisor to CEOs of companies worldwide.

Tor Inge's career spans across several companies, two of which led to establishing Corporater: Equinor (f.k.a. Statoil) — an international energy company, where he held several key positions in the finance domain for over twelve years, and SAS Institute — the largest independent vendor in the business intelligence/analytics market, where Tor Inge spent two years managing the performance management solutions portfolio.

You can reach Tor Inge at vasshus@corporater.com.

Made in the USA
Monee, IL
07 April 2024

56537371R00120